"Ultimate Living"—it is what we all want! Living to our ultimate potential is what God wants us to do. Dee Simmons has put it all together with her life testimony, tremendous victory through Jesus Christ and a progressive health plan that produces a whole person filled with the Spirit of God—body, mind and spirit.

DR. ROBERT A. SCHULLER
CRYSTAL CATHEDRAL MINISTRIES

Dee Simmons has come by her wisdom the hard way, having survived the trauma of a radical mastectomy. But she found true and lasting the importance of nutrition and exercise, and the health-giving power of love and spirituality. Read this moving, courageous and wise book, and use it to take charge of your own health.

BURTON GOLDBERG, PRESIDENT, ALTERNATIVE MEDICINE.COM
ALTERNATIVE MEDICINE MAGAZINE,
AND WWW.ALTERNATIVEMEDICINE.COM

This book, produced by a cancer survivor of remarkable courage, strength and beauty, with its story of her many contributions in the field of health and cancer care and prevention, is a remarkable story and a "must-read."

E. R. ZUMWALT, JR.
ADMIRAL, U.S. NAVY (RET.)

Dee Simmons was a healthy woman in the prime of her life. Then, one day, her entire world shifted on its axis. She was diagnosed with breast cancer. With strength and dignity, Simmons takes us through, first her cancer crisis, then her quest for empowerment over the disease. The result is an informative, inspiring and practical aid not only for cancer patients, but for anyone confronted with a deep need for healing.

ARMSTRONG WILLIAMS
GRAHAM WILLIAMS GROUP
HOST OF *AMERICA'S VOICE* NIGHTLY TV SHOW

Dee Simmons

SILOAM PRESS

Living in Health—Body, Mind and Spirit

ULTIMATE LIVING BY DEE SIMMONS
Published by Siloam Press
An imprint of Creation House
Strang Communications Company
600 Rinehart Road
Lake Mary, Florida 32746
www.creationhouse.com
www.charismalife.com

Unless otherwise note, all Scripture quotations are from the Amplified Bible. Old Testament copyright © 1965, 1987 by the Zondervan Corporation. The Amplified New Testament copyright © 1954, 1958, 1987 by the Lockman Foundation. Used by permission.

Scripture quotations marked NIV are from the Holy Bible, New International Version. Copyright © 1973, 1978, 1984, International Bible Society. Used by permission.

Scripture quotations marked NKJV are from the New King James Version of the Bible. Copyright © 1979, 1980, 1982 by Thomas Nelson, Inc., publishers. Used by permission.

Scripture quotations marked KJV are from the King James Version of the Bible.

Copyright © 1999 by Dee Simmons
All rights reserved
Library of Congress Cataloging Card Number: 99-75004
International Standard Book Number: 0-88419-601-1

This book is not intended to take the place of medical advice and treatment from your personal physician. Readers are advised to consult their own doctor or other qualified health professional regarding the treatment of their medical problems. Neither the publisher nor the author takes any responsibility for any possible consequences from any treatment, action or application of medicine, supplement, herb or preparation to any person reading or following the information in this book.

9012345 BVG 87654321
Printed in the United States of America

Dedication

To the two loves of my life: my darling husband, Glenn, whom I love and adore with all my heart. Thanks for always loving me unconditionally. You're my hero! To my only child, my beautiful daughter, D'Andra, you're the apple of mother's eye.

In Loving Memory . . .
My mother, Mickie Gee, was a passing angel in my life. I miss you so much. You were truly a priceless creation from God as you gave inspiration, blessings and love to everyone. Mother, thank you for teaching me that God never leaves. He is always here—right here with me.

Acknowledgments

Life's most cherished treasures are my true friends.

In friendship and acknowledgment . . .

To Marian Barnes—my very best friend. Thanks for taking care of me when I was ill. I loved all the foot rubs, daily visits and little tea parties.

To Rogene Tadlock—my personal assistant. God knew I need you in my life. Thanks for believing in me and pushing me on. You're truly a dear friend.

To Mike Tadlock—the best cohost ever and also my friend.

To Dr. Joe Godat, Dr. George Peters, Dr. Francisco Contreras—my friends and also my physicians.

To the Ultimate Living staff—thanks for the endless hours you have given to me. You're so special.

To the Ultimate Living distributors who made my vision and mission become a reality—I love you all.

To my dad, Bill Gee, and Joy—thanks for all your prayers.

To Sandra and Bob Glass—my sister and brother-in-law.

To James Gee—my brother.

To Virginia and Ray Stephens—who love me like a daughter.

To supportive friends—like Mary Frances Gibbons who organized my blood bank for my surgery; Dr. Katherine Henry, Pat Wall, Lola Hobbs, Dr. Terry Smith and Ruth, Dr. Karry Barnes, Beverly and Jerry Lancaster, Judy and Paul Thomas, Kay McLeod and Janice Hall.

My heart is full of love for all of you. You have touched my life, and I have grown. Thank you for your support and for being such a wonderful part of my life.

Special Gratitude

To Lindsay and Richard Roberts. I sincerely appreciate your friendship, confidence, trust and continued support. Thanks for always encouraging me to press on. You have taught me to trust God completely. I love your hearts.

Contents

Foreword

George Peters, M.D.

AS AN ONCOLOGIST, I CONTINU-
ally witness the phenomenon
that for most people, cancer
becomes one of the most positive
influences on their lives. Cancer
inspires people to do the things
they really want to do. It changes
their lives in some good ways.

Dee Simmons stands out as
one woman whose breast cancer
experience created a tremendous
difference, not only in her life,
but in the lives of thousands of
others she has since helped and
encouraged.

Dee's modified radical mastectomy and reconstructive surgery took place twelve years ago. I had
advised a lumpectomy, at that time a somewhat new
procedure. Following other medical and family dis-
cussions, however, Dee chose overtreatment rather
than risk the possibility of undertreatment—an
understandable choice.

In those days, breast conservation was still evolving.
Today, the data is much firmer. If we can save the
breast, we save it.

Before her cancer, Dee worked with various charity
and community causes. Today, she works harder than
ever before in her life. She talks to cancer patients
throughout her day. She counsels, prays, encourages
and simply holds their hands. People say, "Dee was
right there with me."

She cares so much for individuals. She is always there
for them—unconditionally. She is never judgmental,
always interested in their well-being. At times when I
have felt low, there was a note from Dee. She makes
you feel as if you're the only person in the world.

This is a book about living—a positive book about
breast cancer. As she shares in these pages, two people
close to Dee died of cancer—but she knows countless
others with cancer who lived. In my office, we get
good news all the time. Every day we celebrate a first
anniversary, a fifth or even a twentieth of someone
who is winning the battle against cancer.

Dee has some very good news to share. During a

long doctor-patient relationship, which has evolved into a mutually respectful and affectionate friendship, we have had only one serious confrontation. That happened just one week after I performed Dee's breast biopsy. I knew this strong, self-assured woman was used to making her own decisions, but I was shocked when a black-tie event came up and she simply removed her sutures.

"That was crossing the line!" I told her sternly.

"I worked for a dentist, and I certainly know how to take out stitches," she informed me. "I sterilized the scissors!"

"Even doctors don't take out their own stitches," I replied.

That's how one stubborn individual met another. Twelve years later, Dee and I stubbornly seek ways to better health and freedom from cancer. We both rejoice at every victory. I believe you will rejoice as well.

Preface

Francisco Contreras, M.D.

You are about to meet Dee Simmons, a Dallas, Texas, wife, mother and businesswoman who works tirelessly with individuals who have cancer.

As a physician and cancer specialist, I often see a certain look on patients' faces. It says, "You never had cancer? You don't understand."

Dee Simmons understands. She has had breast cancer, and the experience changed her. That is why she is so powerful. People who have gone through an experience like hers can make a world of difference in a frightened person's life—and she does, again and again.

Immediately following her own cancer experience, Dee began helping others who had the same battles to fight. Today she does it in a far more organized fashion and has so much more to offer. She visits many patients—and that's unusual.

Proverbs 13:12 says, "Hope deferred makes the heart sick, but when the desire is fulfilled, it is a tree of life." Dee is the personification of that verse. She says, "Hope is there, and I'm going to grab for it." That is very different from most patients who say, "I have cancer. There is no hope." They immediately leave hope behind them.

Dee really personifies that verse. She represents a tree of life. When she desires a good outcome, she works for it and gets it. She is so fulfilled in her life, and she points the way for so many others.

Dee knows a lot about the human immune system, our body's defense against chronic diseases and cancers. She knows emotions play a huge role in how the immune system behaves. Uplifting thoughts and good emotions improve your immunity, while depression lowers it and can make you more cancer-prone.

It is important to take care of a patient's emotional and spiritual needs. Sometimes doctors refer to "the pancreatic cancer" or "the gallbladder" instead of saying "Mrs. Smith" or "Mr. Jones." Patients pick up on that and think, "I'm just a breast cancer."

But when you say, "God is teaching me something. God is looking out for me," even in bad times, the effect on your immune system is positive.

Dee believes, as I do, that even a caring doctor cannot care for you as well as you can care for yourself. She urges you to take charge over your own health and to choose your own medical treatments. Your doctor can give three or four options, but you study those options and decide, "This is it."

We have been taught culturally that the doctor is responsible for your health. However, your health is your own responsibility. As a doctor, I am your consultant. You can do what's best for you, but if you don't believe that, it won't work. As a patient, you should be empowered to make your own decisions. Then you will enter into your treatment with happiness and peace, and you will be far more likely to come out well.

Dee gets close to cancer patients. She is always cheerful. She did what she needed to do to get herself well, and she encourages others to do the same.

A story like Dee's can make an even more profound impact on a patient than any doctor can. This book will affect cancer patients tremendously. I have treated thousands, thank God, with a good success rate, but I truly believe that Dee can impact such people even more than I can.

Women say, "Dee was there for me."

In the pages that follow, Dee will be there for you as well, to bless, comfort and inspire you and those you love.

Introduction

HI! I'M DEE SIMMONS, AND I'M very interested in you. You chose this book because you have cancer, know someone who has cancer or you are seriously concerned for your own state of health or that of someone else very important to you.

Well, you have turned to an expert. I'm not a physician, of course, but I am a healthy, happy woman who survived breast cancer more than a dozen years ago. Believe me, I made myself knowledgeable about that case!

Now it's your turn. I want you to become an "expert" too,

knowledgeable about your cancer or other health issues. I hope you'll learn everything possible about your unique body, mind, spirit and personal health, with the aim of wellness and ultimate living.

Yes, you can do it. There are far more resources out there today than most of us dream exist. This book is written to guide you toward seeking and finding what every person needs most—health, healing and wholeness.

How? By starting where you are this moment. I will begin my own story at that same point—where it all began for me. Come along, and we'll meet some of the most brilliant researchers, physicians, nutritionists and others in the world of healing and wellness. You'll also meet others like you and me...fellow strugglers who met the challenge of breast cancer, heart disease, diabetes or other ailments and decided to prevail. There's a world of good news to discover.

Now, I invite you to meet me in Dallas, Texas, in March of 1987, where my cancer crisis and amazing journey began.

One

The Woman Who Had Everything

MARCH 10, 1987. GLENN HAS A four-day business trip to Germany. This is my opportunity to see Dr. Joseph Godat. I'm having problems, the same gynecological problems that have plagued me for years, and feel sure I'll need another D & C. I'll get this dilation and curettage job done while Glenn is away.

My husband worries about me too much. I've had several of these minor but unpleasant procedures over the years. By now, I take them in stride. However, Glenn always worries.

When I strode into Dr. Godat's office on that beautiful day in early March, I looked like a woman who had the world on a string. As usual, I had dressed fit to kill. *My image demands it*, I thought. Those days I owned and managed fast-growing, highly profitable fashion showrooms in both Dallas and New York City.

Even more importantly, I was, and am, married to Glenn Simmons, a prominent Dallas-based executive who enjoys seeing his wife looking elegant. And at age forty-seven, my long-legged, tiny-waisted frame, tawny hair and high cheekbones still made some people mistake me for a model.

I liked that. Yes, I definitely was the woman who had everything—an adoring husband, a beautiful teenage daughter, a lively social life, a strong place in the community, financial security, closets filled with designer clothes and striking looks that all my life had stood me in good stead.

I had all that, and something more. Unbeknownst to me, I also had cancer.

I really liked Dr. Godat, whom I called "Joe." He had treated my endometriosis and related problems for more than twenty years. I admired his calm, serene manner and enjoyed his quiet sophistication.

Joe Godat by now knew everything important to know about me, I reflected. He knew about the business I founded, about my life, my marriage and my daughter, D'Andra. In fact, I had first consulted Dr.

Godat because of my problems with infertility. His medical expertise had made it possible for me to conceive the daughter I so desired.

As my medical examination progressed that day, I felt grateful that Joe Godat is not only one of the most knowledgeable and skillful gynecologists anywhere, but also my highly trusted friend.

"Dee, you need a D & C," he announced matter-of-factly. "We need to stop this excessive bleeding, and I don't want you to have a hysterectomy. We'll do a D & C…"

"Before Glenn gets home," I cut in.

"Before Glenn gets back. Now lie down again," he gently demanded. "I want to check your breasts."

"No need for that," I objected. "My annual breast exam and mammogram are scheduled for early May at the Susan G. Komen clinic…"

But Dr. Godat paid little heed to my protests. "Lie down, Dee," he ordered once more. I obeyed. After all, it would take only a few minutes.

Almost immediately, I heard Dr. Godat utter a quiet, sharp exclamation. "Dee," he demanded, "How long has this lump been here?"

Surprised, I looked down. On my right breast beneath the nipple I saw a distinct and ominous-looking lump. How could I have overlooked something so obvious? A lump the size of a marble—why had I not seen it before?

Dismayed and shocked, I attempted to joke. "I

guess it popped up between the time I left the house and got here," I answered lamely.

My quip felt flat. Dr. Godat looked disturbed, not amused. "OK, get up. Get dressed. I'm sending you to Dr. George Peters," he called over his shoulder as he hurried out of the room.

I rehearsed my objections while I dressed. I'd had two prior breast cysts—Dr. Godat knew about my fibrocystic condition—and both times had consulted a famous Dallas specialist. Each time the cyst proved benign. So why was he sending me to this doctor I'd never heard of instead of letting me return to the specialist I knew?

"No, Dee, I want you to consult with Dr. Peters," Joe Godat said in a firm voice that let me know, *Case closed. No more arguments.*

I checked into Surgicare two days later at 6 A.M., with my parents accompanying me. I expected an hour's procedure, after which Daddy would drive me home and Mother would get me to bed so I could sleep off the groggy aftereffects. Dr. Godat had handled the logistics amazingly well. He located my preferred anesthesiologist, summoned the heavily scheduled Dr. Peters and even convinced the Surgicare managers to open their facility an hour earlier than usual to receive us.

As the anesthesia swiftly took effect I felt very pleased with the situation. While Godat performed the D & C, Peters would biopsy my breast. Soon my parents would help me into the car, and Daddy would get me home well before noon. And tomorrow, when Glenn returned, I could tell him it was all over and I was fine.

Then I was waking up, gradually realizing that the procedures had been completed. I heard Dr. Godat's voice calling my name as our small, sterile surgery cubicle swam into view, and my eyes began to focus.

Dr. Peters—I had disliked him immediately—now stood in the corner, hands folded, gazing down at his shoes. *He is much too young,* I thought disapprovingly. *Too sure of himself, too. Why is he here?*

It was Dr. Godat who stood beside me, gazing into my face, his eyes filling with tears. "Dee," he said in a voice filled with compassion, "You have breast cancer, but I'm going to take care of you."

I couldn't answer. I looked at Dr. Godat, Dr. Peters and my mother, who now stood near the operating table. One tear slowly slid down my cheek. Mother and Daddy, my precious husband and daughter, dear Dr. Godat and so many other people I loved...this would inconvenience everybody terribly.

I felt no fear, only sadness for those whose lives I would profoundly disturb. Then they wheeled me into the adjoining room where two pastors had been waiting for me to emerge. Through a peaceful, unreal sort of haze, I heard prayers said over me. I could hear my father and mother say, "Amen!"

Still, fear did not intrude. *So much trouble,* I thought again and again. *Such inconvenience for all the people who love me.*

Trouble. Anxiety. Radical change, I thought. I was beginning to imagine what I was about to bring upon Glenn and all the others I most loved.

What I could not imagine that morning of March 12, 1987, was that just as certainly as the sun had risen on a brilliant new Dallas, Texas, day, a shining new life, with a new purpose and calling, was dawning over Dee Simmons.

Who could have guessed that God was about to offer far, far more to the woman who believed she already had "everything"? It still seems impossible to imagine that something as terrifying as cancer actually would become my gateway to a much more abundant and fulfilling life.

Two
_____

Taking Stock

HOW YOU OR I REACT TO CANCER
or any other frightening medical
crisis is as individual as the color
of your eyes—or our life circumstances at the moment of
diagnosis. I have seen some
people react with wild hysteria,
while others exhibit total stoicism.
Betty Rollins, the network television journalist, once wrote a book
about breast cancer titled *First You
Cry*. Except for one tear, I did not
cry. Oddly enough, it didn't occur
to me at the time that my initial
reaction was *strange*.

7

Strange is how most of us feel at first. Everything seems different. Everything is different, and we'd better get past Step One—the strangeness, mental confusion and complex new emotions—and move as rapidly as possible into Step Two—taking stock.

Taking stock means assessing exactly where we are now. It means listing our current assets and needs as honestly and realistically as possible. Only then can we form a sensible game plan. And not to form a game plan spells indecision and chaos.

Of course, none of that occurred to me at first, because Glenn was coming home. Glenn would come through that door and know exactly what to do. He would steer me through the entire cancer-busting process. I honestly felt no fear whatever—just concern that my husband, parents and others might have to suffer because of me.

Sandy, my husband's executive assistant and good right-hand woman, by now had advised Glenn that I "wasn't feeling good," so he canceled his New York City layover and flew straight home to Dallas. He arrived about midnight—more than twelve hours after my procedures—to find me ready, waiting and apparently OK.

As Glenn stepped down into our sunken bedroom, I noted some anxiety on his face. He saw my mother sitting on the bench at the foot of the bed, and me, in full makeup, dressed in my most becoming and glamorous pink negligee, framed against a mound of lacy bed pillows.

"Guess what, honey?" I sang out.

"What?"

"I've got breast cancer!"

"You have breast cancer?" He looked stunned. My happy, expectant facial expression and upbeat tone of voice had led him to expect...what? *She's found a new house she wants to buy, or she wants us to take a trip,* he thought. But cancer!

The news flabbergasted Glenn. Quickly he came to me and put his arms around me, as I knew he would. From within the security of his embrace I answered his questions: "When did you find out?" "Why did you see Dr. Godat?" "What do we do next?" Now that my take-charge Glenn was here, I felt calm and confident, still completely without fear. I knew that Glenn Simmons can handle absolutely anything.

What I had not counted on, of course, was that news of my cancer verdict would devastate my husband. Outwardly, however, he showed no agitation. Looking straight into my eyes, Glenn said, in his direct, low-key way, "OK, I'll close my office tomorrow. I'm going to stay right here with you until we lick this thing."

That was our pattern. Glenn was the answer man. During the dozen years we had been married at that time, he always found solutions for any problem and answers to any questions I ever had. On leaving for work in the mornings, he'd always ask, "Honey, what can I do for you today?"

If I was at wit's end with teenaged D'Andra, who often could be a real handful, Glenn would step in and calm us both with a few good-natured words. (D'Andra is my daughter from a previous marriage. Glenn had two grown daughters by a long previous marriage. He was a wonderful father to all three girls.)

But that was the trouble. Glenn could not step in and "solve" this cancer. He could stand by me, help me, comfort me, *but he could not take my cancer on himself.* That knowledge haunted him. As for me, I was beginning to realize how much I habitually depended on my husband and how little I truly leaned on God. On our fifth wedding anniversary, I recalled, I actually said to my mother, who was my closet friend and the godliest woman I ever knew, "Mom, I know Jesus is the only One who is perfect, but Glenn must be *almost* perfect. I've lived with him five years and can't find a fault in him."

My mother laughed. "Then why don't you just enjoy him?" she teased.

Painfully now, I recognized that gradually I had allowed Glenn to move into the center of my heart and life. He answered all my needs. He cared about anything I wanted to be, do or own. Take my fashion showrooms, for example. Without Glenn, they would not exist. All the beautiful silk blouses, dresses, designer jewelry and couture sweaters... the news articles featuring my success story in *W* and other industry magazines... the lucrative major department accounts...everything I had created went back to Glenn's familiar question: "Honey, what can I do for you today?"

I thought about that day I'd asked the impossible. "Track the designer of this fabulous sweater I found in a Palm Springs boutique," I said. "The label only gives the designer's first name, and I want to order twenty more for friends." All my efforts to contact the designer had reached a dead end. "No, Glenn, these sweaters are terribly expensive. I have to buy them wholesale..."

He came home that same day with the information. Would you believe that first order of sweaters led me to immediate, fabulous success in the fashion business? Me, with no real fashion or business background? *Yes, I owed it all to Glenn*, I thought, *and he is so proud of me...*

God, as you can see, had no place in my thinking. Never had it occurred to me that He might have directed any part of my megasuccess. I had not consulted with Him even once, after all.

Taking stock forces us to ask the central question: "Who is my source?" I had grown up under the example and influence of two strong, faithful servants of God. William Henry Gee, my father, and Mary Maxine McCoy Gee, my mother, modeled the Christian faith and lifestyle before my big sister, Sandra, and me, and later our little brother, James. Because of them I had grown to know and trust God very early, and had loved Him all my life.

Still, incredibly, somehow I had moved away from

Him! In taking stock, the woman who had everything began to face a terrifying truth. Without God at the center of my life, I knew I really had nothing. Nothing at all, that is, of real and eternal value.

Glenn faces problems head-on and tackles them immediately. Early the next day, Saturday, he went into action. First, we needed facts. My diagnosis, according to Dr. Peters, was *infiltrating ductile carcinoma*—breast cancer. By now Glenn had formed a threefold objective: to learn about the cancer and its implications for me, to get a second opinion and to obtain names of the world's top specialists who were most knowledgeable about that specific cancer.

Though Dr. Peters consented to open his office to us that Saturday for our consultation, I still did not like him. Someone in his thirties and so absolutely sure of himself—*arrogant*, I warned Glenn—simply would not do.

I watched my husband interview this doctor. Early stage cancer, he was telling Glenn, every probability of a good outcome after a mastectomy, maybe even a lumpectomy. Lumpectomy? It seemed that Dr. Peters was among the first to introduce this concept, new at the time, of simply removing the tumor with some surrounding tissue. Most doctors believed in the radical surgery.

"What if we don't do anything?" Glenn asked.

"Glenn, your wife will be dead within two years," Dr. Peters replied.

I didn't really believe that. Listening as Glenn asked his final questions, I felt totally comfortable. No problem. Glenn was in charge. He asked Dr. Peters to arrange for a second opinion, then requested a list of the world's top specialists. Glenn did not intend for this young upstart to perform surgery on me. He would take me to Timbuktu, if necessary, but I would have the very best. No wonder I felt so secure!

As we left Dr. Peter's office with my medical reports in hand, it seemed Glenn had still another idea to pursue. He headed his car towards Nancy Brinker's house. Nancy founded the Susan G. Komen Foundation, named for her beautiful sister who died so tragically young from breast cancer.

The foundation, established to raise money for breast cancer research, offers information and encouragement to women suffering from breast cancer, and it raises public awareness about this growing epidemic. It has spread far beyond Nancy's earliest dreams of success. Her Race for the Cure running events have spread from city to city across North America, providing a track record of personal involvement for millions of women in the fight against cancer.

As Glenn and I consulted with Nancy about what might lie ahead for us, to my surprise she confided that she herself had fought breast cancer only a year earlier. She looked radiantly healthy. *If Nancy can handle a mastectomy and look like that, so can I*, I suddenly thought. My spirits began to rise.

She agreed that it's a good idea to get a second opinion before embarking on any sort of cancer treatment protocol. Then Glenn pitched a real hardball across the plate. "Who are the most esteemed and knowledgeable breast cancer specialists in the world?" he wanted to know. "I can take her to Europe or anywhere else," Glenn explained. "I want Dee to have the very best."

"Glenn, I think it's wonderful that you have the time and money and are willing to take Dee anywhere in the world to find a cure," our friend said. "But why go out of the country? Your family, friends and church are all here in Dallas. Your home and your support group are here. Sure, you can find top doctors in other parts of the world, but why do that when one of the most brilliant breast cancer specialists lives right here in Dallas? He's on the cutting-edge of cancer research and surgery. His name is Dr. George Peters."

"Seek, and ye shall find," Jesus tells us (Matt. 7:7, KJV). Taking stock is the starting point, the way to focus on what we most hope to find—the path to wholeness.

I use my own story to illustrate some of the *wrong* paths we discovered as well as the correct ways to get where we want to be. The most important checkpoint, of course, is our relationship to Jesus Christ and our heavenly Father. As I was to learn, even the most wonderful marriage relationship cannot substitute for kinship between ourselves and God.

14

The Bible warns us in Jeremiah, "Cursed is the man who trusts in man and makes flesh his strength" (Jer. 17:5, NKJV). It hurt to realize that I had been leaning so heavily on my wonderful husband that without realizing it I had wandered away from God. Other women I have counseled in recent years have told me the same thing. The answer for each of us is to reconnect with God through prayer, meditation, Bible reading and seeking the presence of God—or to begin such disciplines, even if we have never done them before.

I don't suggest this is a way of bargaining with God for our healing. Rather, it's learning to lean on His strength and power as we enter into surgery, radiation therapy or whatever else may be part of our treatment protocol.

Studies at leading medical centers are showing that the practice of our faith enhances the effectiveness of our medical treatments. That doesn't surprise most old-time doctors who time and again have seen faith-filled patients need less medication, fewer pain pills, sleeping pills or tranquilizers, heal faster and leave the hospital sooner than other patients.

Through prayer we also gain divine guidance— something any cancer patient really needs. I know people with difficult medical conditions who are guided miraculously to the very doctor who perfectly understands their problem and how to treat it. Later they marvel at the time saved by not having to see several doctors in order to find a proper diagnosis.

Prayer helps us into a sort of divine cooperation with our surgeon or practitioner. It gives us confidence as we enter into therapies, treatments and even major surgeries that we understandably tend to dread. Prayer relaxes us and produces tranquility. In fact, it often produces amazing outcomes!

As you go into battle for your life and your health, promise yourself that you'll pray every day. You don't need fancy language, just everyday conversations with God who hears, understands and cares. Lean on Him. Though the rest of us get tired and quit, God never slumbers or sleeps. Even at three o'clock in the morning when the night nurse has dozed off, God is there when needed.

As you take stock, ask yourself how much you intend to invest in your healing process. As I told you, my method was to let Glenn do it—whatever "it" was. What's more, I did not return to my earlier Christian disciplines overnight. Some habits are hard to break. It took a while for me to stop leaning all over Glenn and my parents and begin to reconnect with God.

Meanwhile, back at my parents' home, I knew very well how they would approach my cancer challenge. Mother and Daddy were prayer warriors. They believed in the power of God to heal. I knew Mother and Daddy would storm heaven for what I needed. I also knew they would ask hundreds of other believers to pray for me. I could take that to the bank.

It would have been easy to sit back and expect

Glenn and my parents to do all the necessary praying. Thank God, I did not fall for that idea. Bit by bit, I came to God with my challenges and questions. Soon it became the natural thing to do. An old, good habit was back in place.

Thanks to my daddy, I have always loved the Bible. My father really loved God's Word, and we would often find him reading it during whatever spare time he had after working long hours as a butcher. Daddy definitely was the spiritual head of his household, teaching me and the others by his example while Mother backed him up.

One of my earliest memories is that of his teaching me, as a tiny little girl, to recite the books of the Bible. "Genesis, Exodus, Leviticus, Numbers, Deuteronomy...," I'd begin, as a smile spread over Daddy's face. As I grew up, I came to understand that there are more than seven thousand promises in the Holy Bible, given by God to you and me.

But I got away from those promises and from all the other wonderful revelations in that Book. Now, whenever I counsel another woman who is undergoing her trial by cancer, I refer her to the love letter God has written to each one of us. "Open this book anywhere at all," I tell her, "and you will find something powerful, written just for you."

You ask, "Are prayer and Bible reading all I need to conquer cancer?" Usually not, in my experience. But the Bible tells us that "he gives wisdom to the wise and

17

knowledge to the discerning" (Dan. 2:21, NIV).

I believe that the wisdom and discernment God gives include every important new advance in medical knowledge, surgical procedures and modern medicines. Also, as the founder and manager of Ultimate Living International, Inc., I am convinced that God has made provision for good health through nutrition to people around the globe, in every part of His world.

I'm sold on using this wisdom from God to restore and enhance our physical selves. However, every day I become more convinced that many of us are starving for an even more basic form of nourishment. Long before cancer struck, we were starving our souls. Just as I firmly believe our initial cancer diagnosis requires a second doctor's opinion, I believe our spirit desperately needs an accurate First Opinion—from the living God!

Taking stock of my life all those years ago led me to seek God. God led me to seek His agents—physicians, therapists, nutritionists and others—who helped lead me back to health. Trust me. He wants to do the same for you.

Three

Take Charge!

IN THE TWO WEEKS BETWEEN my cancer diagnosis and my surgery, I was still looking to Glenn's leadership to orchestrate everything. Subconsciously, I believed that if Glenn were facing the facts of my cancer, I could simply concentrate on looking pretty, doing other things and acting as though everything were normal. That way, Glenn, Mother, D'Andra and everyone else wouldn't feel so terrible.

By allowing Glenn to take almost total charge—and he

wanted to, because he couldn't bear the thought of what was happening—I could postpone the hard work of dealing with the terrifying reality. Like Scarlett O'Hara, "I'll think about that tomorrow."

Postponing grief, anger or any other overwhelming emotion may make us look good to others, or so we tell ourselves, but it simply doesn't help. Of course, I didn't know that. So I made sure my two showrooms would run smoothly until my return. I concerned myself with D'Andra and my parents and my household tasks. And I congratulated myself on keeping up a normal façade, one that pleased and relieved our family and friends.

Glenn handled the situation in a much healthier way. First, he cried. Mother said he showed up at her door on the Monday following our Saturday cancer consultations. "He came into the den, fell into a chair and cried like a baby," she later told me. "He said, 'Mickie, I can't live without Dee.'"

Her story surprised me. I had no picture of Glenn weeping, and to my knowledge he never broke down again after that. But having discharged his load of anguish, my husband came home and got to work. Every day he shut himself up in his home office and spent hours praying, reading his Bible, placing phone calls and learning about cancer. He immersed himself in our problem, focusing intently on the job at hand, and committed himself to thorough, intense preparation on my behalf.

As Glenn instinctively knew, you have to *intend* to

prevail over anything that threatens your good health—or your life. This was no time for a timid approach. As you can see, he already had begun our fight, whereas I still just didn't get it! So I allowed my busy work, necessary as it might be, to buffer me against the strong feelings I was so successfully suppressing. Glenn handled all the logistics and guided me through all of our important decisions—except one.

Dr. Godat and Dr. Peters had decided I would have breast reconstructive surgery immediately following my mastectomy. Together, the two procedures would require eight hours of surgery and several units of blood.

"I don't care about reconstruction," I had objected, but the doctors stood firm.

"I know you," Dr. Godat said. "Your appearance is important to you. I know how you dress, how you look and how well you take care of yourself. You need to do this for yourself."

I finally agreed. We chose Dr. Fritz Barton, a neighbor, friend and top plastic surgeon, to perform the breast reconstruction immediately after Dr. Peters completed the radical mastectomy.

Glenn, with our wonderful friend Mary Frances Gibbons, spent hours on the telephone finding mutual friends who donated the blood I'd need. Mary Frances was a professor in the English department at Richland College, and she is one of the smartest women I know and one of my dearest friends. She coordinated our blood bank efforts.

But it was Glenn who engaged a luxury suite for me at Baylor University Hospital, Glenn who hired private-duty nurses to care for me and Glenn who, at last, walked with me down the long, silent corridor that leads to surgery.

No wonder I was able to dodge fear so well. My husband took all possible fear and distress upon himself and did it gladly, as he always had.

No one else could take away the post-op pain, however. That relentless pain felt exactly like a Mack truck parked on my newly slashed chest, an unbearable weight just sitting there, refusing to move. I was lying against another lengthy incision, tying to understand why they had cut my back. Later, I learned that a sheet of skin from my back had been harvested so Dr. Barton could make my new breast.

I had to lie inert, though I longed to turn on my other side for relief. Nurses insisted that I must not move...I should not risk tearing any of those crucially important stitches. As the pain reached one crescendo after another, I begged for painkillers, which at times were refused.

Every two hours or so, a chaplain would enter the darkened ICU and pray with me, yet the pain did not yield for even a second. Hour after hour throughout my blackest night, the darkness swam with my raw pain. Feeling hopelessly weak and sick, it was as though an endless succession of savage beasts were attacking me all night long, without mercy.

Never had I felt more defenseless and alone.

That night I did not dream that I would someday hold the hands of countless others as they battled through their own rendezvous with cancer.

The weakness, pain and nausea followed me as they rolled me into my hospital room, which was filled with flowers and nearly as lavishly appointed as a bridal suite. Fifty or more friends milled around in the adjoining room, each one wishing he or she could help. Prayers surrounded me.

But I felt encased in sickness and pain, hardly aware of anything beyond my own miserable body. Mother was there, and Glenn, and Marian Barnes, my closest friend in the world, trying so hard to believe I was OK and looking so subdued and white-faced.

The telephone rang, and Marian sprang to answer it. "She's too sick to talk right now," I heard her tell the caller.

"Just put the phone to her ear," I could hear a voice say.

"Dee, this is Carlton Pearson." His voice crackled with energy. Carlton is a family friend, a beautiful, dynamic Christian minister.

"Listen carefully, Dee. I want you to know that God is going to use this experience in a powerful way. Everything you are going through right now is going to be used in your ministry to others."

I can't imagine how, I thought, as I thanked Carlton and let Marian hang up the phone.

I relate these experiences as a backdrop to what God was about to show me, and what I have since been privileged to share with thousands of others. Meeting me at the weakest point of my life—perhaps you see your situation in exactly the same way—God was about to capture my full attention, then my most serious thinking and finally my total obedience. Soon I would turn my back on my fast-track lifestyle.

A Fork in the Road

Soon I was home again and recuperating in my pretty bedroom. I was healing steadily. Cancer is not exactly a walk in the park, but there I was. The pain was still very much with me, but this too will pass...

Actually, some wonderful events occurred during the week I was in the hospital: the gorgeous bouquets, literally too many to count...precious Marian, standing at the foot of my bed those times when I hurt the most, rubbing my feet by the hour...and, most amazingly, the incredible moment when the doctors removed my surgical dressings and I saw my new breast. It looked impossibly authentic, exactly like the one it replaced, except that we'd have to wait for final healing before they could construct a new nipple.

Very few women are so blessed, I realized. Most endure the trauma of seeing a bright pink scar on that flat place where a breast used to be.

Day after day I begin to see and marvel at how blessed I have been. I smile when I think of the new friendship between Dr. Peters and me. I had come to see how honest he is, and how compassionate. Faced with the agonizing wait for results of lab tests that would tell if my cancer had spread—and if additional treatment would be needed—I begged Dr. Peters to inform me the moment he got the word.

"But I'll probably be in the operating room when that happens," he objected.

"Can't you have someone hold the phone for you while you tell me?" I begged.

"Sure. I'll do that. I know how much suspense you're feeling," he said, his voice suddenly compassionate and kind. He was as good as his word. He telephoned from the operating room—and the news was good!

At home, things resumed as usual. By phone, I learned that my showrooms were doing well. I could relax. Each day I dressed myself in pretty nightwear and carefully applied my makeup before beginning my day's "recuperation duties." Soon Marian would arrive with her tea tray, Earl Grey tea to brew in a silver pot, and a selection of exquisite teacakes for us to nibble.

She'd pop a classic movie into the VCR. The two of us would prop up on my big bed, watch Clark Gable and sip our elegant tea, feeling like young girls at a house party. It was a wonderful, happy interlude.

One day a seemingly random thought changed everything for me.

"It's time for you to take charge," I heard myself say

to myself. "Only you can heal yourself. Glenn cannot do this for you. *Take over!*"

I sat up in some excitement. I had come to a major fork in my life's road. On one path was all I was so accustomed to—tea parties and pampering, loving parents and friends and a doting husband.

The other path deserved real exploration. No more depending on Glenn and others for what I could—and should—do for myself. My mind raced. Could I actually discover the cause of my cancer? Could I rebuild my good health? More importantly, was I willing to make that commitment to myself—and stick to it?

Yes.

Anyone Can Learn to Be Healthy

Mother raised Sandra and me, and later James, by *The Book*—Dr. Spock's book. That meant cream of wheat for breakfast, no fat, very few sweets, and no meals after 5 P.M. My mother wouldn't dream of allowing us to eat junk food!

When I refused to eat my cream of wheat, Mother would make me sit there until I did eat it, even if I were late to school. Sometimes Grandmother would take pity on me and wash the sticky stuff down the sink.

This produced two tall, thin, healthy and energetic girls. We yearned for forbidden fruits, however. We found ways to sample the things my mother kept away from us—and we enjoyed our hidden moments of self-indulgence.

I have always been interested in food, but never much interested in nutrition—before cancer, that is. That little girl who once sat down and ate a stick of butter grew up to be a woman who enjoyed a dozen cookies each morning with her first cup of coffee. That's before breakfast! Also, while I'm confessing, I might as well tell you these were serious cookies, with double amounts of chocolate chips and nuts.

You and I know exactly where we fail ourselves in the good health department. We also lie to ourselves about health issues. *Nothing wrong with those cookies, or even with eating a whole pie,* I told myself, because I kept my twenty-one-inch waist, no matter what. Luckily, I inherited Daddy's metabolism. He never carried an extra ounce on his frame, nor did I.

Deep down, I knew my diet was terrible.

Slowly, carefully as I began to take charge of my own health, I realized I could learn how to be healthy.

So can you.

Why Cancer? Why Me?

As I thought about my experiences, I began to wonder why I had gotten cancer. What had led to it? Even doctors can only guess. My cancer may have taken years to develop. As I questioned myself, I thought of several possibilities. Those years I had worked in a dentist's office—was I overexposed to radiation? Or was it secondhand smoke? Or was it all because of my unhealthy diet?

27

Whatever the cause, we should not beat ourselves up and blame ourselves for past failures.

Be kind to yourself. Blaming never helps. Get over it. Ask yourself, *What is my responsibility now?*

Cast Out Blame

It's important to repeat this point. We must actively cast out every desire to blame ourselves or others for a cancer condition.

We can't afford to bog down in negatives. We need to focus on moving ahead toward healing and wellness. Take a moment to decide whom you will not blame: yourself, your mother, your boss, your P.E. teacher, the U.S. Army...You get the picture.

Sometimes bad things happen to good people. There's no need to blame anyone at all.

Learning and Growing

We learn a lot from dealing with a life-threatening disease. We learn about bad health, good health and what we want to do about each.

We can grow into a wonderful new lifestyle, if we wish. (I learned I could get along just fine without all those cookies.) We can start today.

Instead of feeling *condemned* to adopt a fat-free diet or forced to take up regular exercise, we can look at the positives:

- I can learn how to become lean and mean.
- I can make my muscles well-toned, whatever my age.
- If I lose even five pounds, I'll improve my blood pressure.

There's plenty of good health news out there if we care to hear it. Use what you know, and you literally can turn back the clock by ten or fifteen years!

My Responsibilities

We know what they are. We really do, and we know it's far more important to walk every day or lose ten pounds than to buy another life insurance policy.

I am responsible for myself and for my own health and well-being. I am responsible to my spouse and my children, to my boss and even to my dog. I know I am irreplaceable. How responsibly do I care for, protect and enhance a person as valuable as I am? The same is true of you. How well do you care for, protect and enhance a person as uniquely created, as valuable, as you?

I had to determine to change my diet. I had to determine to exercise regularly. I had to determine to become as healthy as I possibly could. Just as I wouldn't think of skipping brushing my teeth for a week, so I could no longer drift along, neglecting proper nutrition and exercise for days or weeks at a time. It isn't enough to look good; we must also be healthy if we are to know ultimate living.

Create Real Health

I am creating my physical, mental and spiritual self this very minute. We all are. Question: Is this a passive exercise in my life, or am I proactive?

As you know, we can reverse bad health and overcome bad habits. For instance, if you stop smoking today, five years from now your body won't know it ever craved tobacco! And with proper nutrition, plaque buildup on arteries can recede and blood vessels become supple and strong.

Small steps add up to desirable gains. Walk an extra block, go to bed an hour earlier or skip the ice cream. It all starts with your decision to begin noticing the little things.

Day by day we create a lifetime of good health and vitality. Anyone for tennis?

Nurture Yourself

Why are we so ashamed to admit our secret desire for more nurturing? Within our heart of hearts, we yearn to give ourselves the best—the care-taking each of us deserves.

What's stopping you?

Perhaps we're too proud to take an afternoon nap and ruin our Superman or Superwoman image.

Maybe turning off the television and giving yourself a whole day of blessed silence would restore your soul.

Or maybe it's time to buy yourself a new mattress

and pillows. What one thing would best help you nurture yourself? Why not give yourself a gift?

Doing My Best for Me

It is time to find solutions to long-standing problems and focus on finding real ways to improve my health.

I create my own circumstances. If I write a check and join the health club, I will be likely to use it. If I get out of bed an hour earlier, I can start my day with a walk. If I choose and eat five fruits and fresh vegetables each day, I am helping to prevent cancer.

Teeth in good repair. Yearly eye and hearing exams. Improving my posture. Treating myself to a long swim or massage. I need to create the habit of giving myself the best. I deserve some respect!

What Makes Me Happy?

Radiant joy and happiness bespeak maximum good health. What's more, they can be downright contagious.

Ask the next three people you meet what they do to make themselves happy, and note the response. Huh?

Happiness doesn't just happen. It begins when we decide it's necessary and desirable for ultimate living. It's the occasional gourmet coffee treat, thirty minutes in a hammock, exploring a flea market, playing dolls with your daughter . . .

Make a list. Write down one happiness source for each year of your life, then pick a number.

Remember, even with a broken leg, the flu or in the midst of cancer therapy, real people find ways to be happy. Perhaps I can't do a lot about my disease, but there's plenty I can do for my spirit.

Four

The Love Factor

I ABSOLUTELY LOVE DR. GEORGE Peters. By now you've guessed the truth: that initially I had transferred my hidden fears and dismay about breast cancer onto the brilliant oncologist we'd chosen to treat my cancer.

That's really not an usual reaction. After all, no one wants to undergo a mastectomy, even to save one's life. And while I did not outwardly protest the diagnosis—I actually acted fairly unconcerned about the whole cancer thing—my subconscious feelings at first created some negativity about the man appointed to save my life.

Fears we don't acknowledge or confront certainly complicate things. The coldness and arrogance I thought I saw in George Peters actually were nothing more than a perfectly normal professional, confident demeanor. And as for his youthfulness . . . well, it was actually beside the point in that his peers already recognized him as foremost among the world's authorities on breast cancer.

So why do I share this story? Why confess that I was wrong about my doctor? Simply to say this: Fear sometimes chooses very inappropriate targets. What's more, fear usually distorts our perceptions.

Fortunately, there's a powerful antidote to the gut-level fears that dive-bomb us when we hear the word *cancer*. The answer is love. Love is our first line of defense. These next pages contain stories of those who discovered that love represents an essential element of our healing. We need to recognize that fact early on. And once we choose to face everything about our situation with the dynamite of love, we can blast most fears into fragments!

As cancer patients often tell me, our capacity for loving others and allowing them to love us increases dramatically at those times when we need it most. It's as though God stretches our heart and fills it with that peace that passes all understanding—far beyond anything we know in ordinary times.

Sick or well, of course, we need to actively cultivate our abilities to love and be loved. But when we become physically challenged, love empowers us to walk through the fire of radiation therapy and not be burned. And love provides patience—day by day, hour by hour—when we face lengthy or unpleasant treatments or procedures.

God's wise, enabling love also helps us to keep our eyes fixed on the unique person, instead of the cancer. Embracing this love allows us to focus on the best possible outcome. And it teaches us to believe, as the saying goes, "I have cancer, but cancer doesn't have me."

Love Thy Doctor!

Once you choose the specialist who will partner with you in seeking your healing, it is important to ask your spouse, family and other prayer partners to pray for him or her regularly. Your doctor or doctors will diagnose, prescribe treatment protocols, perform surgery and oversee rehabilitation. He or she will guide you through these steps, and possibly others. Your chosen doctor will follow the outcome of your treatment for years to come.

Your doctor-patient relationship will become a long, intimate and, ideally, a cordial one. It will emerge as one of the most crucially important team efforts in your life. Needless to say, the earlier a godly, trusting partnership can be formed, the better.

One man tells about walking into a world-famous

cancer treatment center and discovering that the physician assigned to his difficult case was "a woman doctor who looked all of seventeen years old!" He says he wanted to flee. Instead, the man drew a deep breath and told his physician, "We know this is a tough case, but my wife and I are praying for you. Everything will turn out fine."

The patient watched the young specialist's shoulders relax. Her face lit up with a broad smile. "Thanks," she said. "I believe in that." Doctor and patient bonded strongly at that moment. Months later the man completed his treatments. He was sent home—with a successful outcome few had believed possible.

What part did love play? No one on earth can say. More and more leading physicians believe, however, that love, which leads to faith, and faith, which leads to inner peace, all seem to play an integral part in attaining restored health.

I always held great affection and respect for my doctors. My breast cancer experience, however, convinced me that fondness and friendship are equally as important as trust. Take Dr. Godat, who had treated me for years prior to the day he told me I had cancer. We'd always had a great doctor-patient relationship, but that day I had impatiently protested against his taking time to do the breast exam he thought he should do.

"I have a mammogram appointment just two months from now," I argued.

But Joe Godat later told me he had an inexplicable,

gut feeling that he should examine my breasts, despite all my protests. Of course, he then discovered the tumor. How dangerous it would have been to wait another eight weeks before treatment!

I also love Dr. Godat for referring me to Dr. Peters. Both doctors have my deepest gratitude for insisting that I have breast reconstruction. They actually decided that for me—a risky thing to do—because they realized that I was not yet processing the facts well enough to know how to decide.

Had I had an arm's length relationship with either, there would have been a different outcome. Both men, however, involved themselves in my psychological, as well as physical, welfare. They were willing to steer me to the answers both believed I would ultimately want, and I thank God that they did.

My love, gratitude and respect, of course, extends to Dr. Fritz Barton, the plastic surgeon whose genius created an amazing breast replacement following the mastectomy, and to Dr. Frank Coufal, the anesthesiologist I always want to attend me. These gentlemen are the best. Each has become my friend, as well as a highly trusted physician.

And as for Dr. Peters, time and again he has extended himself toward the people with cancer I have been privileged to counsel. So often I have turned to him on behalf of others. He always cares, and always comes through.

How could I not love my doctors?

Person to Person

People say medicine has become so impersonal these days. "What if I can't choose my own doctor?" they ask. "And what if he or she turns out to be the coldest, most hurried person on the planet? What if I really don't like him?"

My prescription: Bombard your practitioners with prayer. Tell your doctor you intend to place your faith in his judgment and expertise. In short, always reassure your doctor, nurse or therapist. If she draws blood skillfully, tell her she's good at it. While waiting to see the doctor, write down the questions you need answered, and tell him you want to save his time after the appointment. Write each one notes of appreciation. Little by little, show everyone in your medical world that you are not just another medical problem, but a real person who appreciates each person in the office.

Remember, these are stressed-out human beings who often bear tremendous, even overwhelming, responsibilities, day in and day out. These people come to work early and stay late. If a patient unexpectedly requires surgery, his doctor may have to postpone his own vacation. And many forego taking a lunch hour. There simply isn't enough time.

Do these professionals need and deserve our love? The answer is obvious. Each time we take a minute to cut a rose for the nurse-receptionist's desk, or to say a sincere "thank you" to the x-ray technician, we humanize our healthcare system a tiny bit. Whenever we visit a doctor's office or any other medical facility, we might ask God to show us who needs our encouragement most. There's always someone.

Loving Friends

If your pre-op plans called for the prayers of loving family and friends, you know what it's like to go into surgery with that indescribable feeling of perfect calm and peace. No man-made tranquilizer or sedative can give you that.

Everyone who faces surgery should experience that feeling. The good news is, anyone can. Glenn and I so appreciated the wonderful friends who crowded into the hospital room adjoining mine, people who had come to pray. They prayed, and they stayed. They were faithful. Even at my sickest, I could feel their prayers surrounding me.

Such love humbles us. We are helpless, and we need other people's support. We need to know that countless hands are there to bear us up. And if we have sickness or pain, those hands remain close by, ready to stroke a feverish face or an aching back. Knowing these things works wonders—even while we're under anesthesia.

But what if you have absolutely no one to pray for you when you become ill? That question haunts some people—especially the elderly, widowed, physically handicapped and chronically ill. It haunts even healthy young people who have moved to a new community and feel alone.

Fear not. Whatever your circumstances, you will discover an amazing fact: You have friends you do not know you have. They always find us, because God has promised He will not leave us comfortless. Here are some ways to help yourself or someone you know—or don't know—who finds himself alone, ill or afraid.

- Contact a church of your choice and ask for a minister or priest to visit. Most large hospitals have chapels for patients and their friends. Simply ask. Someone will gladly help you find whatever you need.

- Ask to have your name placed on a prayer list. Countless thousands, probably millions, of prayer chains exist, so many, in fact, that you or your loved one might even receive around-the-clock prayer.

- Be gracious and receptive to those who offer to sit with you or your family. Don't say, "My surgery is too early in the morning. You really don't need to go to that trouble." Don't deprive that person of the blessing he or she will receive by serving you. This is the time when we need every bit of the love that is offered.

- Ask for a Bible. Most nurses can find a Bible for you. Hotels and motels have Bibles in every room. Read from the Book of Psalms for courage and comfort.

- Realize that God will not leave you alone at a frightening time. Even if you've never prayed before, He is as close to you as the mention of His name. He will provide someone for you, even if you fall sick while traveling far from home. Remember, God knows exactly where we are.

At Your Side

My husband is the strongest man I know. Even more importantly, Glenn is a strong Christian. You cannot shake his faith. When he kissed me just before I entered surgery, his calm strength enfolded me, and I felt no apprehension whatever.

But even the strongest man needs a friend beside him at such times. Glenn has several close friends, but Jerry Lancaster was the one who showed up during the wee hours of that morning and simply sat with Glenn. That's the way men do things: just sit together, drink coffee and talk about nothing in particular. Jerry Lancaster helped my husband, and I love him for it.

Marian Barnes poured herself out in service to me and truly shared my suffering. I told you how she rubbed my feet, all she could think to do when I had

41

so much pain. I could feel warmth from her precious hands through those old bed stockings they make you wear, and I literally felt her love. Marian stayed with me. Jesus used her heart and her hands to comfort me.

We need to be willing to watch and wait with the friend who needs our love and prayers. And let us be ready to accept that same healing love from those who want to watch and wait at our side.

Family

When you can absolutely count on your family, as I always could, eventually you come to realize how much their loyalty and love empower your healing. And once we realize that, we need to go on and become family to others who are sick or incapacitated and need our encouragement.

These facts hit me hard while I recuperated from surgery. Once you leave your fast-track existence and lie in bed for a few days, God can drop a lot of old memories and new thoughts into your conscious mind. Sometimes, I began to see, you need healing for more than just your body.

I kept remembering things about my hard-working daddy, for example. I thought of how he'd let Mom buy those cute, ruffly dresses for Sandra and me, dresses with skirts so full they stuck almost straight out. Meanwhile, Daddy would be putting cardboard inside his own shoes with the worn-out soles.

Daddy and Mother were humble, sweet people, but

maybe they felt a little pride when people commented on their two pretty little girls. Daddy would smile and say, "Thank you," then look straight at me and say, "Pretty is as pretty does."

He needed to remind me. Sandra, whom I always looked up to and admired more than any other girl I ever knew, was a hard act to follow. Sandra not only was a brilliant, conscientious scholar, but she excelled at everything else she did. She gave our parents absolutely no trouble, as I remember, but willingly helped Mother around the house, made top grades and even sewed her own clothes—beautifully.

By contrast, I was a tomboy, always getting into trouble, and certainly never felt willing to stop and read a book. My grades? Never mind! Daddy and Mother were strict with me, but patient.

One thing Daddy would not tolerate, however, were my antics in church. I sat up front with my girl-friends. Daddy looked down on us from his place in the choir, behind the pulpit, and he could see every-thing I did. Often he'd catch me giggling, pinching or bouncing around in the pew. Then he'd leave the choir and suddenly there he'd be, leading me out to the parking lot for a spanking.

Daddy also took the lead in teaching me to love the Bible. He worked hard at slowing me down long enough to teach me the things that really matter. I remember one Sunday night when I stayed home from church because I had the flu. I was maybe ten years old.

Daddy heard me crying when they came home, and hurried to my room.

"What's the matter, Diane?" he called out.

"Daddy, I need to be saved."

He must have been surprised, even shocked. He sat with me that night, talking, questioning and explaining, until he had satisfied himself that I truly understood what I was about to do.

Then he and I knelt beside my little bed, and my daddy helped me pray the sinner's prayer. "Jesus, I know I am a sinner and that You died for my sins. Please come into my heart right now. I want You to be the Lord of my life."

The Lord reminded me vividly of that holy moment and the precious experience I had shared with my father. Other times, my mother's face came to my thoughts. Daddy and I may have shared the same looks and strong nature, but mother and I shared the same heart. She and I were far more than just mother and daughter. As anyone who knew her would agree, Mother consistently set such a shining example. No wonder I had always loved everything about her!

Mother took my childhood badness in stride. She'd get angry when I misbehaved or got into trouble at school, and she'd also get exasperated when I'd talk my way out of my well-deserved punishments. I always was secure in her love; no matter what I did or failed to do, she was always was by my side.

Mother also was able to love Sandra and me for

who we were. She did not throw my big sister's successes in my face or compare my behavior to Sandra's. What wisdom! I never felt my parents loved Sandra more than me. I grew up proud of my sister, and I always loved her. Today she is a highly successful professional woman who lives in Virginia. I wish we lived closer to one another!

God also was reminding me that I had wandered away from my strong religious moorings. I had grown up, left our working-class neighborhood and married a wealthy and successful man. God blessed us and our marriage. And though we were church-goers, pray-ers and generous givers, nevertheless I had gradually allowed glamorous fashions, exotic vacations, the rush of top business success and a life of luxury to intrude on the daily intimacy I once had known with Him.

I knew God was beckoning me back to a closer connection with Him. The question was: What did I really want?

Help others? I already had everything I wanted in life. What more could I possibly want? And where did I fit into anybody's idea about helping others?

Love Yourself

Once we see how much God has loved us, and how much others have loved us, the next big question arises: Do I love myself?

Some of us women become shopaholics. You see the career shopper lunching at nice restaurants with her

45

overloaded shopping bags parked at her well-shod feet. She's wearing real gold jewelry, not costume stuff, with her Chanel suit. Most people would say, "How indulgent. Obviously, she loves herself."

But excess never equates to healthy self-love. We all know women who would not even dream of wearing artificial pearls, but who settle for a purely materialistic and artificial life. Sorry, but if we truly want healing, health and wellness, we must do a lot better than that!

And that includes me. I wince to remember how much food I used to pile into my mouth. D'Andra, like most young daughters, often found her mother embarrassing. When we'd eat at our favorite cafeteria, she would cringe as I helped myself to three desserts. Chocolate, coconut cream and butterscotch pie . . . why not? I stayed slender as a reed. How can you argue with a tall woman who stays a skinny size six?

One night, dining out with Glenn, I ate one meal and then ordered a second one. When I finished that, I had my usual three desserts. A man strolled up to our table and spoke to Glenn about this.

"I've been watching your wife eat," he said. "I've never seen another person eat that much. How can you afford to feed her?"

"Well, I don't take her out that often," Glenn deadpanned.

Glenn is funny, but my self-destructive habits were not, I realized. My mother insisted that her family eat right. Once I left home, however, I began eating junk, junk and more junk. I ate anything and everything, from morning to night.

Recovering from cancer surgery, wondering why I had cancer when most of my friends did not, I guiltily took stock of just how reckless my eating habits had become. My mind ranged far and wide as I considered how crazy my life was becoming: yo-yoing between two major merchandise marts, stressing out over buyers and accounts, snapping at my daughter over everything.

I sure have my faults, but I am honest with myself.

"I've got to make a decision, and this is what I must decide today," I told myself. "Do I want to live, *or do I want to die?*

"Glenn cannot do this for me. My doctors can't do it. My mother and father can't make me well, nor can D'Andra. I'm the only person in the world who can take charge over this situation . . . and I will."

That day I began to love Diane "Dee" Simmons—to love her enough to honor her truest needs. I loved myself enough to change my priorities. And I loved myself enough to begin exchanging the good, or at least the glitzy, for a more centered, spiritual and satisfying life.

We must love ourselves back to health. We must learn to love others, and receive their love fully. This decision marks the beginning of our journey back to health and wholeness.

If it does nothing else for us, our cancer experience at least should teach us to treat ourselves with respect. Learning to love ourselves, I now understand, not only teaches us how to love others, but also to more fully love the One who created you and me.

Five

The Healing Desire

I BELIEVE WE KNOW DEEP DOWN exactly what we need to do, or not do, to promote better health, or even healing, for ourselves. But we must ask, "What do I intend to do about it? How far will I go in my efforts? How much do I actually *desire* my healing?"

The day we receive a cancer verdict is the day we hear a very loud wake-up call. Any of us who have heard our doctors pronounce the "C" word remember the numbness and sense of unreality that swept over us then. Cancer? Me? Unthinkable!

Certainly the word *cancer* no longer necessarily means the end of life. These days most cancers, especially when caught in early stages, can be treated successfully and vanquished. But every cancer, whether or not doctors can establish a primary cause, points to one indisputable fact: Our immune system is faulty. Our body's defenses are low.

Now the ball is in the patient's court. Does she really intend to push toward the goal of ultimate living? Is the *desire to win* rising up in her now, ready to work in her favor? This is the life-or-death question, probably the most important we'll ever face.

MYTH: Once you find the top specialist in the field relating to your cancer and follow his instructions to the letter, you have done your part.

FACT: That statement is fine, as far as it goes. But *something* has made your body let down its guard and destroyed your immune system. Let your physician provide the superb treatment and care you deserve, but realize that *you* are the best possible detective to track down the cancer-causing culprit and arrest it.

Testing Our Desire

"I'm the only person who can make me healthy," I sometimes tell people. No, I am not discounting doctors. Dr. George Peters, one of my closet and most trusted friends, would be the first to agree that doctors *treat*, but God *heals*. Even those who do not believe in a personal God can readily understand that our will to participate in our healing—a burning desire to battle this thing and win—breathes life and strength and some intangible element of extra oomph to our doctor's finest efforts.

In other words, get an attitude. Boost your desire. A woman asked, "Pray that I can stop smoking cigarettes."

"Do you want to quit?"

"No," she admitted. "I really don't."

All the prayer in the world won't overcome that woman's lack of desire. And all the best medical knowledge and prayer aren't going to fix a body that's totally malnourished—one that's habitually fueled by three desserts at one time! I must desire to overcome the tiredness and lethargy and other bad effects those sugar binges brought on.

I am not saying that pie causes cancer. I am saying that most of us honestly know where we're not doing our best. And all of us can get even more honest and ask: "How much do I really want to give myself what my body needs?"

In a loving way, some of us also need to ponder this: What do I get out of being so sick? For many, illness may be the only way they can allow themselves the attention, rest or sympathy they need. Others may be suffering from clinical depression.

Our desire to know the truth about ourselves becomes a honest basis for seeking the healing we claim we want. No back-and-forth about it. No "one step forward and two steps back." Desire leads to single-minded commitment!

A woman tells me about her scary medical diagnosis, and I ask, "Did you get a second opinion?"

"No, my insurance won't cover that," she answers.

She passively accepts whatever her primary physician and her insurance company tell her. She even argues with the idea that she might need that first diagnosis verified, or disputed, if only for her own peace of mind. That next logical step—a second medical opinion—would cost perhaps one hundred dollars.

"Is your life worth one hundred dollars?" I ask her.

The woman looks surprised, and then nods, smiling. She is catching on. If there is one message I want to get across, it is that we occupy a physical body that is literally priceless. It amazes me that men who wouldn't dream of taking a Rolls-Royce to the village mechanic for a tune-up do far stupider things to the finest machine ever created!

Where We Place Our Energy

Look where we place our energy, and you know what we truly desire. At the time of my cancer surgery, most of my energy was dispatched to my fast-growing business in two of America's most important fashion markets—New York and Dallas.

The kind of major success I was experiencing would intoxicate almost anyone, man or woman. I did not need to earn a living. The business had started small, with a little boutique behind Glenn's office where I sold accessories—good-looking belts, handbags and so on. It was my hobby.

I'm really not a hobby person, however. I'd rather throw myself into the venture and give it all I've got. Soon I discovered those fabulous sweaters I mentioned earlier, and Glenn tracked down the designer. The twenty expensive sweaters Estelle allowed me to carry got snapped up immediately. Soon I was outselling Estelle's top sales reps and urging her to give me my own territory.

One thing led to another. The more money I made for Estelle, the more generously she mentored me. She taught me how to enter the big leagues of the fashion game, and I taught myself everything I could about the industry. In an amazingly short time I was able to lease showrooms in merchandise marts with waiting lists of two to four years.

The sky was the limit! The more I ventured, it seemed, the more I gained. I carried only top lines with the market's highest price points. It was incredible to see a gal with no business experience, and certainly no background in high fashion, learn what I had to learn as fast as I had to learn it. Meanwhile, money simply poured in.

What did all this effort cost me? Nothing, monetarily.

I had seen nothing but good profits, and I felt very proud of myself.

I had a lot of flash, but very little self-esteem at that time.

When I married Glenn Simmons I was thirty-four, a multiple beauty-contest winner with a divorce behind me, and I had an adorable little girl to raise. Glenn and I felt such an immediate, magnetic attraction toward one another, and we developed such a deep love that it seemed we'd never need anything more.

Then came that "hobby," which became so enormously successful. I loved telling reporters from *Women's Wear Daily* the secrets of my success! Work and making tons of money can easily become addictive to someone with low self-worth. God wanted to show me those things.

Now when I counsel people with cancer, I often begin by asking if they have experienced any major crises during the past eighteen months.

"No-o-o," they always say. Then soon they begin to realize where they have stretched their energies, sometimes nearly to the breaking point. They begin to get the picture.

It is so painful when we begin to realize how, through our own excessive actions, we may have cheated our own lives and short-changed those we care about most. The fact is, each one of the thousands of cancer patients I have counseled has recalled that their lives endured some terrific strains during the two years prior to a cancer diagnosis. We literally seem to stress ourselves to the physical breaking point!

For Glenn and me, marital problems never became part of that picture—"Thank God!" I always added. All too frequently, however, I meet cancer patients whose energy has been consumed by toxic and troubled relationships. But Glenn and I were building a big Texas house—a mansion, truthfully—that stressed us both. Even happy stresses work against our immune system, we now know.

"Tell me what has happened in your life. What kind of tragedy? What has upset you? What bad event?" I ask people with cancer.

"Nothing. Nothing," they say. Everywhere in the world I go, I get that same response.

"OK, let's go back," I tell them. "Think really long and hard. Has anything affected you emotionally during the past two years?"

I wait, and then it spills out. They lost a loved one . . . endured a divorce . . . financial problems . . . heartbreak over a child. Even the little children I talk with can describe painful events in their lives.

Only God could possibly measure the amount of physical and emotional energy—energy that represents life itself—that all of us pour into absorbing emotional pressures. It does not take a trained psychiatrist to figure that out.

The thing is, we move so fast and juggle so many responsibilities at one time that there's no time to process emotional issues, even deep grief, properly. A *Wall Street Journal* article described how large corporations treat executives who have experienced emotional upheaval—the death of a spouse, for example. Bottom line, these people are expected to keep a stiff upper lip. Some women managers and CEOs who become pregnant actually hide the fact as long as possible, then work from home, and return to the office just days after they deliver.

We move too fast. We don't stop to count the cost. We spend our physical, emotional and spiritual energies with abandon. We act as though there will never be a payback time.

My own fast-track life had collided with D'Andra's needs during the months prior to my cancer diagnosis. My daughter, by then a turbulent teenager, became inexplicably—and unacceptably—rebellious. I believe a lot of her pain over her parents' much earlier divorce finally surfaced.

We had talks, arguments and professional counseling, to no avail. Finally, D'Andra went to live with her biological father for a few months.

What a relief! For six months Glenn and I had a chance to enjoy our marriage and each other. I told all my friends how wonderful it felt to return to sanity. (I know a lot of women who read this will say amen.) But while I was smiling and joking on the outside, each day I was dying a little more on the inside. You can imagine all the various emotions I was stuffing down. Meanwhile, I did not acknowledge to anyone, most of all myself, how much grief I was feeling about D'Andra.

The house we were building . . . my booming business . . . troubles with my precious daughter . . . these things did not directly cause my cancer. Little by little, however, those months of heavy emotional expenditures helped break my immune system's bank. My body had little strength with which to fend off marauding cancer cells. I was a sitting duck.

Good News

We can rebuild our frayed immune defenses. That's the good news. The rest of the news, however, is that it will take honest work, honest desire and honest effort to do so.

Test yourself: Where have you lived emotionally during the past twenty-four months? If this has been a dynamic and happy period in your emotional life, good for you. Keep it going. If your emotions have slid off the deep end at times, especially in combination with heavy overwork, illness or other physical stress, pay attention. Remember, our bodies are amazingly resilient until we grossly overload the system.

Healing mechanisms are build into you and me well before our birth. These are part of our individual genetic design. They come with our basic defense package. When we keep this primary immune system reasonably strong, we quickly recover from the colds, flus and infections everybody experiences. The maladies nobody ever expects to get—like breast cancer—normally get rebuffed.

But suppose cancer already has arrived, and someone you love is battling against it. The good news is, there are some potent ways for a person to improve his health while he fights off the aftereffects of radiation therapy or chemotherapy. Recent discoveries, particularly in the field of nutrition, can help us strengthen the physical body even when its immune defenses obviously have been knocked to its knees.

Perhaps the disease was caught late. Doctors are pessimistic. The outlook seems poor. There is still good news for anyone who desires ultimate living. First, no doctor can accurately predict the length of anyone's life. Doctors can only offer an educated guess usually based on statistics. We all know how often these well-intentioned guesses wildly miss the mark.

The good news is, God knows exactly how many days, months and years you and I can expect to live on this earth. Our job is that of fulfilling each day to the best of our ability. It is up to us to desire health—genuine, overflowing, abundant health—even in the midst of sickness and pain.

And there's more good news: You can do it.

As you read further, I pray that some of the reports from other cancer survivors and the ways we can triumph over deadly disease will renew your own desire for a health profile filled with energy, stamina and wellness.

The day I climbed out of my bed and declared, "Nobody else can do this for me. I'm taking charge!" was the day my own desire for excellent health took hold.

They say that the place you focus your vision becomes the place at which you arrive. I looked toward radiant, vigorous good health, and thankfully, that's where I am today. I desire those same blessings for you.

Six

Something More

THERE'S NO TIME LIKE CONVALES-
cence to make a woman close to
God. Resting, healing, attempting
to return to normalcy; nevertheless, time seems to come to a
near-standstill, and thoughts and
good memories crowd in when
you least expect them.

With my housekeeper and
Marian there, I had all the help
and diversion any woman could
need. And then there was
Mother. She stayed close by me.
I didn't even have to ask. It
would not occur to my mother
not to be there.

As Mother moved about,

answering the telephone or the door, arranging flowers or bringing me a fresh outfit to put on, she certainly did not hover. But something about the presence of this tiny but spiritually powerful woman redirected my thinking and soothed my spirit. She had that effect on most people.

My mother always had modeled a life of the highest integrity, morality and compassion before me, my sister and our brother. When I was three, my parents dedicated me to the Lord at church in Dallas. My parents became pillars of that full-gospel church and dedicated themselves to their children's Christian rearing and education.

For Mother, that meant quietly living her life with excellence. She did everything well. God gave her the gift of love—far more love than the usual maternal feelings. She poured her love over everyone in her circle of influence, and we all responded to it. She had a cute little habit of tucking love notes into your lunch sack or under your pillow or in a pocket. She wrote thousands of those little notes to me—I still have hundreds—and to everyone else whom she could encourage.

So here I was, convalescing, with this beautiful little woman, so loving and cheerful, constantly with me. Mother's very presence continually turned my thoughts to the Lord—because that was the realm she occupied. I knew that very well.

I liked it that she always dressed so beautifully. By

nine o'clock in the morning, she would have tidied her house and gotten dressed and ready for whatever business the Lord might assign to her that day. Now I was her assignment. Here she was with me, in her nice pants suits, her pearl earrings and her hair looking perfect.

Whether or not we talked, Mother and I always communicated. Whenever she passed my bed she'd lean down, smiling, and pat my face . . . and later, I'd find a tiny piece of paper on my night stand or somewhere, with a message:

"You will never know God is all you need until God is all you have."

Or, "Tender, loving care means a hug, a kiss, a prayer."

How I loved my mother!

I had chosen Glenn as the man I most wanted to marry when I was only seventeen. I didn't know this highly successful older man, of course, or move in the same social circles. I merely worked in the dentist's office where he brought his two daughters for their dental check-ups. He was strikingly handsome, I thought, with prematurely silver hair against a tanned face. His good physique, ready smile and caring way with his little girls made me fantasize about being married to him.

But Glenn was married, and not to me; I was much too young for him even to notice. Still, he stood as the prototype of the man I wanted some day—handsome,

wealthy, successful, gentle and kind. I could imagine
how he would shower me with luxuries and attention.
He would adore me, and I would be the happiest
woman in Dallas.

Silly, girlish dreams? It's hard to know. Suffice it to
say, I still worked in that same office when Glenn's
lengthy and turbulent marriage came to an end. I had
no way to know any of that, however, until circumstances suddenly threw us into conversation, and later
we made a date for lunch.

That first, random date has lasted until today. Our
first conversation, which electrified both of us, has
never stopped. The life I imagined, fantasy stuff, came
true all right, but with so much more. Glenn courted
me for two lavish and exciting years before we decided
to marry.

Mother was no meddling mother-in-law, understand. Here was a wise and godly woman who knew
her daughter and respected the man she was about to
marry. She could see down the road. She knew that
unless we put God first, there would be a human colli-
sion ahead. My mother knew how crazy about this man
I was, and she could see why. She loved Glenn, too.

So Glenn and I started attending church together
and have done so ever since. The foundation for our
marriage, and for healing the broken places in our lives,
had been established. Glenn is a natural leader, and
Mother's words to him made perfect spiritual sense.

After we set our December 6, 1975, wedding date,

the tests began (Glenn said that November 6th, my suggestion, wouldn't do, because every anniversary would fall during hunting season.) One night Glenn came to my house, walked in my front door and immediately began to get something off his chest.

"I have to tell you something. When I tell you, I know you'll break up with me," he began.

"What, Glenn?" I couldn't imagine what would make him talk that way.

"I have no more money."

"Well, go to the bank and write a check," I said.

"You don't understand," Glenn told me. "There is no more money. I have lost it all. The stock market fell, and I lost everything. I have enough for two weeks, and then I'll have to file for bankruptcy."

Slowly it began to sink in. The unthinkable had happened. Neither of us could believe it.

At that time, Glenn played poker every Monday night with some of the wealthiest businessmen in Dallas. Stakes were high . . . far higher than I could imagine. Not that it mattered, since Glenn habitually walked away with more money than he lost.

My mother told him one day, "Glenn, you're going to church now and trying to serve the Lord, but, honey, you can't gamble. It's not scriptural."

"Mickie, there's nothing wrong with my gambling," Glenn argued. "After all, I keep a record of my winnings, and I always tithe."

"Well, Glenn, I'll tell you what. I'm just going to

pray about it, and let's see what God says. If God says it's OK, that's fine," she told him.

The next Monday night, Glenn lost. Accustomed to winning large sums, that night he lost every penny he put up. After three consecutive Monday nights of losing, he quit. To this day he has never played in another poker game.

The following Sunday morning Glenn phoned me and said, "We're going to church. Where do you want to go?"

"I don't care," I told him.

"We're going to find a full-gospel church," Glenn informed me. He was beginning to want the kind of faith my mother had. We slid into the back row of a church that morning, and when they passed the offering plate Glenn placed everything he had in it. Later he told me he had offered God a prayer: "I'm not asking you to give back the wealth I had. If You will restore to me even a portion of what I had, I will never cheat You out of another dime." He has been faithful to that promise since that day.

That week Glenn got by, and he did not have to file for bankruptcy. The next week, God began to restore what had been taken away. From that day forward, God blessed Glenn mightily, both financially and in the far more important areas of life. God saw Glenn's sincerity and honored his prayers.

Before we married, we had both committed our-selves to serving God. A dozen years later, recovering from breast cancer, I recalled those events as though they had just happened. They were part of a tapestry of memories that was emerging, often due to something or other my mother might recall.

"Remember those baptizings, Diane?" Mother always called me by my given name. Daddy usually called me "Di," and Glenn had named me "Dee."

I could quote the scriptures when I was a little kid, and good preaching really impressed me. Funny, I had almost forgotten those Sunday nights at church when I would preach to a whole room full of other kids. I wasn't tall enough to reach above the pulpit, but I would stand there and preach.

During the following week, kids would come to our house, and I would baptize them. At the foot of a hill behind our house there was a creek where I immersed these children, and afterward, the dogs and cats. I knew the seriousness of what I was doing. It was very real to me.

We'd have tent revivals in our back yard, with me preaching and praying over those other very young boys and girls. There actually had been an anointing over those early revivals, I now realized. Strange . . .

Then I was growing up, becoming a pretty woman and a flirt, leading boys on, accepting their engagement rings, teasing, manipulating, always promising, yet remaining a good girl. Baptism ceremonies gave way to beauty pageants, and Mother and Daddy didn't understand all that.

I was past twenty years old when I began using makeup and entering beauty pageants.

"You have natural beauty. You don't need makeup," Mother always told me.

But I never had many nice things, so I entered the pageants to win the prizes. My parents didn't fuss or argue with me, but they never came to even one pageant. That hurt a little. There was not one picture taken of me in those contests in which I was smiling.

Those days, I thought I was finally beginning to look fabulous. As I perfected the outside, however, I completely overlooked the inner person. Little by little, I painfully saw that I had competed for man's trophies and failed to see what God wanted me to win. No wonder I did not look or feel really happy.

Little by little, discontent crept in. The driving urge to have things—a radio, sharp clothes, my first car—all quite normal, of course. Later I wanted the handsomest man in Dallas, and got him. Next I wanted a baby girl . . . and, thanks to Dr. Godat's medical know-how, could finally achieve that dream . . . and then, it seemed, I really didn't want marriage at all.

But without God to guide my life, how could I have known what to want? Mother and Daddy had watched my years of struggles and mistakes and loved me anyhow. They adored D'Andra and always helped when she got colicky or asthmatic and I didn't know what to do. They had stood by me always, regardless of my failures, just as Mother was standing by me now.

During those days of recuperation, as I waited for incisions and cut nerves to heal and sutures and drainage tubes to be removed, day by day another invisible but far deeper healing was taking place in me. I believe many women experience this while recovering from breast cancer. The hidden, undealt-with parts of our lives now surface. We begin to understand some of the powerful emotional influences on our physical bodies and the role these play in our sickness and health.

As Mother moved through my life while I rested, remembered and healed, I began to appreciate how often she had gone face to face with God during decades of prayer, intercession and service. Mother had wrestled with many difficulties, including a late pregnancy in which she had nearly lost baby James. I could only imagine the prayers that had surrounded my little brother when she successfully brought him to term.

There are many things to endure that are as hard, or even harder, than breast cancer, I told myself. As my mother moved about in my room, I gradually began to comprehend the Source of her remarkable strength and beauty.

Within two weeks after my hospital exit, I was invited to my husband's office for a small private lunch with Dr. Robert Schuller. As we finished our time together, Dr. Schuller came over and took my hands, prayed with me and told me, "God will use this as a ministry for you. You must come and share your testimony on my Sunday morning *Hour of Power* television program." Only two weeks, and I was given the "ministry" message for the second time!

Maybe that's why, when my church had someone call me with an invitation to give my testimony at the Spring meeting of the Women's Ministry, I did not turn them down. This happened just two or three weeks following surgery, and I really had not yet regained my strength. True, I was healing well, but it still seemed like strange timing. I was shocked at myself for accepting.

Glenn by now had returned to his office part time, and Mother and Marian were resuming their own routines. I was coping with my surgical pain pretty well and was looking forward to returning to my own job.

I accepted the invitation. Then doubts swept over me. I could not speak in public, especially to two hundred women. I just couldn't do it. One on one, on the job, I could sell anything. It did not faze me to walk to the owners of the ritziest stores in America and convince them to carry my clothing lines. If I believe in something, I can sell it.

But I can't speak to an audience, I told myself. I felt a little sick. Here was a woman who looked so poised and self-assured, but I knew that was a lie. Inside, I quaked at the thought of public speaking. I wouldn't enter a pageant today, I realized. I wouldn't have the talent needed to win. I would be afraid to walk out in front of people. I never wanted to speak in front of the public. My knees would shake . . . I would feel insecure and inadequate . . . not smart enough . . .

Yet there I was, standing in my bathroom and putting on my makeup, on the Saturday morning before I am to speak to those churchwomen. Suddenly, I find myself speaking to God. "You know I really don't understand this . . . why I had to go through this . . . why You allowed it.

"Could You just let me know, God, if there's anything that will come out of this cancer? Are You going to get glory from it?" I had never questioned Him this way before. I had not gotten angry with God or said, "Why me?" Before now I simply had asked myself, *Why did I get cancer, when I thought I was so healthy?* If possible, I just wanted to know why.

As I stood in the bathroom in my stocking feet that morning, I immediately heard God speak to my questioning heart. "This will become a ministry for you. You will minister to people around the world."

Ministry? Carlton Pearson had used that word. I did not understand, but there was no time to figure it out or question Him further. I finished dressing and went right out the door.

Praying hard, I got up to speak to the women at our church. Out of my mouth began to flow streams of living waters—because I was anointed, because I knew

God was speaking through me. I had expected nothing of the sort. I could hear myself testify, could feel that amazing inner calm, fully knowing as I spoke that these were not the words and thoughts of a scared, stumbling woman, but words richly supplied by our loving God.

This is what God means by ministry. You go in obedience, and He gives you what you need, as you need it. This humbled me. I felt the real awe you experience when you receive a specific revelation.

Back at home in my familiar kitchen with my husband, that amazing experience still followed. I could not even explain to Glenn what had happened. I could not explain it to myself, for that matter. I only knew I had passed some kind of test and that my life had turned a corner.

Later, Glenn and I had a conversation that I will never forget. "Honey, sit down," I commanded. "This is it. I am taking charge. I'm going to work this thing out," I told him, meaning the "cancer thing."

I wanted Glenn to know my intentions—that from that day on, I would take responsibility for my good health. Then, an inexplicable thing happened. For no reason I can explain, I walked over and opened a bottom cabinet drawer. Inside I found a bottle of something I had never seen before—some kind of green powder.

Now, I know my house. I can tell you where everything is. But here is this unfamiliar bottle, in a drawer

I never use. Why had I even opened it?

It was a mystery to Glenn, too. But somebody had put that bottle there, with a sheet of paper telling a story titled "It Really Happened to Me." It was a story about a woman's cancer and how someone had sent her this green powder . . . and she got well.

What a strange day. Hour by hour, God had gotten my attention. He had it now, as I stared at the mysterious bottle of green powder and the paper that accompanied it. I had no idea how either item came to occupy that cabinet drawer, and I never did find out.

My discovery, however, like so many other discoveries I'd had in recent days, was to change my life forever.

Seven

Self-Defense

I DIALED THE LADY'S FORT
Worth, Texas, telephone number
with great anticipation. There
was a woman healed of cancer,
according to the news story I had
found so mysteriously. Her name
and telephone number had
appeared in the article, and it
didn't take long for me to contact
her.

"You don't know me," I began,
and then proceeded to tell her
about the green stuff I had discovered in my kitchen drawer.

"Oh yes, honey, let me tell

you about it," she exclaimed. We developed an instant friendship as I discovered she was a Christian, eager to tell me all about the virtues of that green powder—a near-miraculous supplement she believed had restored her health.

We talked on and on. She related story after story about other cancer-afflicted people who had benefited from this and other supplements. Her accounts fascinated me. I had paid little or no attention to nutrition since I grew up and left my mother's nourishing cream of wheat. Our conversation provided the first inkling I had that illness sometimes—many times, according to her—could be turned around by adopting a good nutritional regimen.

That is old news these days, but during the mid-1980s it was still a somewhat revolutionary and controversial idea. I had never wasted my time with "health nuts" in the past, but that was BC—Before Cancer. Now I was ready to listen.

As I told Glenn what I intended to do, I began to take charge. I found a Dallas health-food store and bought a juicer and a couple of books on alternative healing methods. Unwittingly I had walked into one of the best health-food stores around, and immediately I began to be tutored by the owner, Yvonne.

At that time, of course, I didn't even know what a one-a-day vitamin pill was. I knew absolutely nothing. But God favored me, and my education process began.

Vaguely I had begun to understand that rebuilding my health would be largely up to me. My doctors had played their roles superbly. Now I must take over where their expertise left off.

As I listened to Yvonne, and later began to read, I learned there's a lot about the benefits of nutrition that few doctors have been trained to utilize. It soon became clear that there was a lot of information out there that could enhance my cause. Without really intending to, I had taken my first baby steps on a fascinating, ongoing journey.

At that time I had no idea that thousands of other women, and numbers of men, later would join me on the way.

Rebuilding the Walls

Entering into the job of restoring my health reminded me of the Old Testament story about Nehemiah's rebuilding the broken-down walls and burnt-out gates of Jerusalem. Shocked at the destruction, and fearful for the vulnerability of Jerusalem, Nehemiah courageously determined to rebuild the city's walls. This took some twenty years, beginning in 445 B.C.

Something like Nehemiah's shock of dismay had happened to me. My human walls—the immune system—had been broken down. Like Nehemiah, I felt great fear. So I had gone to my knees before God and, like that great Old Testament leader, had become determined to rise up and rebuild.

75

But first, the Old Testament account goes, the city had to be cleansed of the evils that had crept into its daily life. As you saw in the preceding chapter, I had to begin that same process in my own life. Through prayer, rest and remembering, God brought to my mind some "evils" that had to go. Some seemed like such small things—dietary indiscretions, for example.

Then there was my fast-paced, no-rest lifestyle and the way I recklessly squandered my energies. My fashion business had largely accounted for that. Despite having a staff of nine, plus one fashion model, our large sales volume meant constantly increasing responsibilities for me.

I knew I must close that incredible business. Only after I shut the door firmly against the clamors of the fashion world could I begin to rebuild myself. That was a big decision. I decided to keep the business going only until our leases expired, thus giving my team time to find new jobs. It turned out that acting on that decision was surprisingly easy.

The only really big thing I had to confront before my healing could begin was my painful, apparently no-win relationship with D'Andra. "Where was I failing her?" I asked God that question a thousand times as the chasm between my daughter and me continued to widen.

Why, when I had my surgery, did the girl choose to go on spring break at South Padre Island instead of staying with me? I could not understand that at all.

76

Later, in counseling, D'Andra and I confronted that painful issue.

"Mother, I could not deal with your cancer," D'Andra said. "I lost my father when you divorced. You gave me a wonderful stepfather, and I love him, but I had lost my father. I was afraid that now I was about to lose my mother, too."

So the poor child went away, hoping she could put me and my cancer aside for a few days. She was so frightened she could not bear to face it.

Now, during our face-to-face session with a trained counselor, D'Andra said, "Mother, I'm standing here today asking you to forgive me. I abandoned you. I deserted you when you were going through cancer surgery because, Mother, I couldn't handle it. I was thinking, 'Now I'm going to lose my mother.'"

That day began a great healing in our mother-daughter relationship. Our wounds were cleansed. Love was expressed, and we began to rebuild what I had feared had been nearly torn down. Children do grow up. My only child has grown into a lovely and very loving woman—and best of all we are great friends.

The Process

I discovered that there are many good books written about breast cancer. Soon books about cancer prevention, nutrition and alternative medicine were stacking up in our house. I read everything I could get my hands on, asked a million questions and learned everything from how to use a juicer to how to figure out my own dietary and diet supplement needs.

Glenn, always agreeable with whatever I plunged into, tolerated my new enthusiasm. Soon I had him taking that great green powder, plus a bunch of other supplements I recommended. However, he refused to read any of my nutrition books or even discuss the subject very much.

"Just put them out there, and I'll take them," he said, referring to my current crop of nutrition aids. As always, he was good to his word. He did take the supplements and did not do the reading.

I always plunge myself up to the neck whenever I study anything new. I ate, slept and talked nutrition. I began meeting more and more people who were interested in the subject. I think of my fashion business, which began at ground zero and climbed to the stratosphere as I learned more and more about that far-out industry. Now I was just as determined to learn absolutely everything there was to know about vitamins, free radicals, antioxidants, trace minerals and everything else, but there was a big difference between knowing everything about *fashion* and knowing everything about *wellness*.

At first I did not understand that it's not necessary to choose between conventional and alternative medicine. I was seeking every kind of alternative, looking for magic bullets. The best approach, of course, lies in taking the best of science and the best of nature.

Balance is essential, as I was about to learn in a most dramatic way.

Charlene

In July, following my surgery in March, I was sitting in a doctor's waiting room when a woman walked in. I stared at her, and she stared at me. We were the same height and build, and we had the same high-fashion look. It's a shock to see your twin!

As it happened, we walked out of the office at the same time. Impulsively, I spoke to her. "You are so gorgeous!" She said, "I was thinking the same thing about you.

"I love the earrings you are wearing," she continued. "I'd love to have some like them."

We then introduced ourselves, and I promised to order her some earrings like mine. Then we walked toward our cars, and they were twins! Each of us drove a black Mercedes convertible. We had matching cars.

I couldn't get Charlene Calvert out of my mind. I told Glenn about her when I got home, and I went immediately to order the earrings she wanted. When they arrived a few days later, I had to phone more than once, because Charlene was determined to pick them up when I was home. We seemed drawn to one another. We were incredibly alike.

Charlene finally drove up in her little convertible

one day, top down, her elegant silver hair blowing, and she seemed to radiate extraordinary beauty and health. When she walked into my living room, the place lit up. Imagine my surprise, then, when within five minutes of conversation I was somehow confiding in her that I had had breast cancer.

"When?" she asked.

"Last March."

"I had breast cancer surgery, too," Charlene said.

"When?"

"In April."

I simply stared. We had cancer surgeries just one month apart. What's more, as our conversation progressed, we discovered we had very similar experiences, except for different doctors and different hospitals.

Soon Charlene and I went all over Dallas together, the closest friends imaginable. She was in the real estate business, divorced and in love with a wonderful man. A physician's daughter, Charlene was as interested as I in finding answers to our medical questions. We began to read the same books and attend the same seminars. We not only were researching, but also wanted people's survival stories. How did they survive? What did they do to make a crucial difference in their lives?

Charlene and I not only looked alike, we were alike. She was as aggressive as I when it came to research and interviews. We read everything and studied everything we could get our hands on. We enjoyed learning. We were always interested in getting out and finding answers.

As we bonded and studied together, we became interested in macrobiotic diets—mostly vegetarian, low fat, with natural grains, beans and nuts. This became widely accepted as an effective anticancer diet. We ate nothing but the best natural foods.

Together, Charlene and I spent the next year absolutely devoted to getting ourselves well. We worked hard to rebuild our immune systems. I had learned very quickly what a free radical was and what an antioxidant was. Here was a woman who last year had been totally ignorant about all that. Now I could reel off facts like a pro.

Charlene and I learned all about nutrients and how they work in your body. We learned about eating. We studied about the effects of exercise. We learned about every alternative approach imaginable.

In short, we tried just about everything, including treatments we discovered in other countries. We were ignorant enough at times to try things we should not have tried. However, I thank God that Glenn could afford to allow me to travel, study and find my own answers. I was intelligent enough to check out treatments and decide whether they were valid. I would ask others, "Did they work? Did you get results? Did this or that help your life?"

However, people get into trouble when they do what Charlene and I were doing—pursuing one wild mix of one "cure" after another. After all, if one thing didn't work, another surely would! A couple of times, tests revealed high levels of tumor markers in my body . . . a scary thing.

One time I returned from another country after a round of treatments with a suspiciously high blood level of something that made Dr. Peters anxious.

"What have you done?" he demanded. "I know you. You have done something."

"No, I haven't," I replied. Actually, I was using tons of things. Certainly I didn't have the nerve to tell George Peters I was taking hundreds of dollars worth of pills each month!

One thing I like about Dr. Peters is that he sees you regularly throughout the first year following your cancer surgery, and almost as much the following year. During those visits he'd sometimes get pretty angry with me. "I don't care what you do as long as it's not going to hurt you . . . and as long as someone's not taking advantage of you," he'd tell me.

Charlene and I, meanwhile, would congratulate ourselves because were becoming healthier and healthier. She was always happy. Everything always was great. If it were going to storm outside and a tornado were going to hit your car in the next three minutes, she'd say, "Oh, honey, it'll probably pass on by your car."

Those first two years of our friendship I'd sometimes ask her, "Charlene, why don't you get all the tests my doctor gives me? I don't understand this. Dr. Peters makes me come in every three months."

"I don't know why your doctor insists on seeing you so often," she'd say. Then I'd get mad and ask, "Dr. Peters, why do you make me come in so often? My best friend had cancer only one month apart from mine, and her doctor doesn't make her come in."

"Dee, that is her doctor's business," Dr. Peters would insist. "My patients are going to come."

One snowy, cold day the phone rang, and it was Charlene. "Dee! You're never going to believe . . ." she began with a laugh.

"What?"

"You won't believe what my doctor just told me," she continued. "Dee, he told me he thinks I have lymphoma!"

About that time she said, "Hang on. There's a cop with his flasher, and I'm going to get a ticket." She pulled over to the side of the road, got her ticket and returned to our conversation.

"Can you believe he thinks I have lymphoma, Dee?"

"Charlene, come to the house right now," I told her.

How was this possible? Here we are observing this macrobiotic diet. How could Charlene have lymphoma?

Within moments Charlene walking, smiling broadly and complaining about the treatment her famous doctor wanted her to take. "I'm going to fight this 100 percent alternative, Dee," she announced.

After two years of studying alternative medicine, Charlene no longer believed in chemotherapy. She did not believe in radiation therapy. Unless it were holistic medicine, Charlene did not believe in it.

"I'm going to fight this," she assured me.

"Charlene, I don't know what to do," I answered.

Now, here's an important thing to remember. I have never told a person what he or she should do. If someone asks me how I handled my cancer, I tell him. If he asks me what I'd do if I were in his shoes, I always reply that I cannot answer honestly because I am not in his shoes.

"We're going to fight this," Charlene repeated. "We're going to go further into the macrobiotic diet, and . . ."

I just panicked. I got on the phone and called George Peters. He had never met Charlene, but I said, "George, you've heard me talk about my good friend, Charlene? She has seen a doctor who believes she has lymphoma," I told him. "George, would you come over to the house tomorrow and see Charlene? Would you sit down and talk to us?"

The next day, Saturday, Dr. Peters drove up through blowing snow in the same little car like mine and Charlene's. Both he and Charlene had a hard time chugging through the thick snow, but somehow they got here, and we sat on the den floor in front of a roaring fire in the fireplace.

Charlene explained to Dr. Peters that she did not

intend to pursue any ordinary medical course, but planned to fight her battle with alternative methods. "Will you help me?" she asked him.

I knew Dr. Peters as the soul of American Cancer Society conservatism. What a question to ask him!

He immediately began to talk to Charlene and offer suggestions on different treatments and therapies. He too saw that she was going 100 percent alternative. No turning back.

"Charlene," he told her, "I do not agree with what you're doing, but I will be there for you. And if you *do* need me to come in if this gets really bad, I will."

I watched my friend begin to travel, seeking the wildest treatments you can imagine. She traveled thousands of miles, spent thousands of dollars and grew sicker and sicker. From time to time she would check in with Dr. George Peters, my oncologist. They became fast friends.

Charlene always managed to joke about her condition. "I'm going to beat this. I'm going to *whip* this," she'd say. My heart grew heavier and heavier as I watched her steady decline. Dr. Peters took care of her at times, as he had promised. He removed some large tumors to give her some relief. And when she needed a medical doctor to admit her to a hospital, George Peters would always help her.

Meanwhile, Charlene refused to eat one bite of food that would not be classified as strictly macrobiotic. It is true that diet is widely acknowledged to be cancer preventive. A severely restricted diet regimen does not provide adequate nutrition for certain cancer patients. Additional vitamins and minerals, antioxidants in particular, are valuable additions to that rigid diet.

But Charlene did not vary from her stringent diet. She also had turned away from the chemotherapy treatments her oncologist strongly advised. After trying many alternatives to chemotherapy, at last she turned to a medical facility I had visited in Mexico after a nutritionist I respected introduced me to the owner. Dr. Francisco Contreras, who had followed in the footsteps of his physician father, was noted and respected for his creative and compassionate approach to treating cancers. Dr. Contreras had visited Glenn and me in Dallas, and we had hosted a party so our friends who were interested in his work could meet him. He also toured Baylor Hospital at that time.

It's easy to like this handsome, warm-hearted and humble physician. His beliefs in modern medicine's state-of-the-art treatment protocols combined with certain alternatives—relaxation techniques, nutrition and, above all, reliance on God—impressed us as uncommon common sense.

Charlene agreed. I traveled with her to Mexico, and soon we were settled comfortably in her hospital suite where I would remain for the first week of her two-week stay. By now Charlene's condition had become so grave that IV tubes dripped into veins day and night. Dr. Contreras confided that they would do everything possible to make her more comfortable, but he held out little hope for recovery. They would remove some of the largest tumors by surgery.

The week wore on. Charlene's high-spirited attitude could almost persuade visitors that everything was fine. She laughed and joked with nurses and attendants, but after they left the room she'd whisper, "I'm so tired."

I could see that my friend was dying.

The morning I was to leave Mexico, as I prepared to shower, I happened to look in the mirror and saw something that struck a cold terror into my heart. Two nodules had suddenly appeared on either side of my body—exactly as Charlene's now desperate condition had first revealed itself.

Dear God!

Glenn was flying in to take me home to Dallas. In my numbness and shock I decided to tell no one about the nodules. Once home, filled with indescribable panic, I telephoned Dr. Godat. He saw me immediately. Afterward Dr. Peters checked me as well. My two wonderful doctors agreed on a course of powerful antibiotics. The nodules remained for two years before they slowly vanished.

My deep-seated fears lasted even longer.

The Prayer

By the time Charlene returned home a week later, I had begun to withdraw from everything. Charlene telephoned me regularly, but I could not make myself go to see her. Suffering intense fear, grief and depression, I began to lose weight. Within months I went from my normal size six to wearing a size zero. Dr. Peters found no physiological reason for all that.

Glenn and Mother became increasingly concerned, of course. At last they persuaded me to see Dr. Rick Fowler, a marvelous Christian counselor who listened as I poured out my emotions and fears.

"You think you are going to lose Charlene, and you can't deal with it," he commented.

By now Charlene's other friends had begun to phone and tell me Charlene was asking for me. I would explain that I didn't feel good enough to leave home. At last Dr. Peters said, "Dee, Charlene is really bad. You'd probably better go see her while she's still home."

I fled straight to Rick Fowler's office that beautiful sunny day. "What am I going to do?" I wept. I could not stop crying.

"You must go see her," Rick said. "You know she is dying. Unless you go to her, you will never be able to live with your guilt feelings.

"Let's pray right now," he suggested. "Afterward you're going to leave this office and go straight to Charlene."

We joined hands and prayed. Then I got in my car and made the fifteen-minute drive to my friend's house. My heart filled with dread as I drove. Once there, Charlene's nurse ran out to greet me. "I'm so glad you came!" she kept exclaiming.

The windows were up, and the day's brightness and fresh breezes poured into Charlene's house. As I walked upstairs I silently prayed, "God, I can't do this. I can't stand it." Then I entered Charlene's room, where she lay huddled in bed, pale and weak, but still smiling.

"Hi, honey, how are you?" she gasped, coughing and straining for breath. I knew her lungs had begun to fill with fluid.

"Charlene, don't talk. Let me talk," I ordered.

Many times in the past I had talked to Charlene about a personal relationship with God. "I'm a Christian," she would always say. At that moment, however, I felt in my heart that Charlene really was not ready to meet her Master face to face. *I just knew.*

"Please don't talk. Let me talk," I urged. "I have a question I must ask you."

"What, honey?"

"Charlene, are you ready to go home to heaven? If you were to die, are you sure, without a shadow of a doubt, that you are ready to go?"

"Yes," she answered.

"Charlene, I have to know," I pleaded. "I have to have that peace beyond all doubt. Would you repeat this simple prayer to God after me, telling Him that you're trusting in Jesus as your only way to get to heaven?"

"Oh, yes."

I began to pray. God's presence came all over us. She sat there with her eyes closed and repeated every word. When we stopped praying, Charlene reached over and took my hand. Tears filled her eyes.

"Thank you, baby," she whispered.

After sometime, I turned around and walked out. By the time I descended the stairs and walked to my car every bit of that burden, that unspeakable heaviness, had left me. God had lifted it off my shoulders.

Within hours Charlene was transferred to a hospital room. Our visit had been my last opportunity to see her alone, I realized. Friends trooped in and out of her hospital room, and—here's something funny!—when I visited her next, she asked me to bring her a chocolate pie and a lemon pie!

A few days later my beautiful, smiling "twin" left this world to enter God's presence. I was devastated. It seemed impossible that someone so full of life and wonder, someone who noticed and appreciated even the tiniest little flower, could not whip her cancer after all.

Charlene's death also devastated Dr. Peters. They had become such good friends. Once again I had an opportunity to see the real empathy and deep compassion of this man.

Answers

I returned to my nutrition studies, lonelier than I had ever been before, but now so very determined. The last months of Charlene's life had changed me drastically. I had become as thin and gaunt as if I were terribly ill. My grief seemed relentless.

Gradually, however, peace began to enter my suffering heart. God was beginning to show me how intensely I had identified with my valiant friend. I had taken on her anxieties, her steady weight loss, even my nodules mimicked her physical experiences. It seemed as though, in that identification, I had actually tried to enter into Charlene's skin and share her battles.

It was no wonder, I thought. *You could not have placed a knife blade between Charlene and me. We had become so close.*

God used that friendship's closeness and human identification—yes, and heartbreak—to give me some important insights. Heavy-hearted and deeply grieved as I was at what some might see as the obvious failure of diet, nutrition and alternative medicine in Charlene's case, by now I knew far too much to turn back.

As I returned to my studies during the months following Charlene's death, my thoughts returned to her often. During those same months my body weight steadily returned to normal. God was guiding me in other profound ways, as well. He had brought me to understand fully two crucially important truths:

- Conventional and alternative medicines should not war. Each enhances the other. I believe intelligent people should seek a balance, accepting the best of science and the best of nature.

- Some cancer patients choose to place their entire faith and hope for a cure in medical science alone. Others place every shred of their faith in receiving a divine intervention and healing from God.

We need both. We need the best that modern medicine can offer. But above all, we need God—His mercy, His guidance and His love.

Eight

New Power
and Purpose

"Is anyone there with you?"

"No. Only my secretary."

"Please close the door and go in a room by yourself," the unfamiliar voice instructed me. *Why?* I wondered, but I did as he said. A very well-known American doctor was at the other end of the telephone line. Why was he calling me?

"Tell me what an antioxidant is," he began . . .

This doctor was not the first who had called me for information. Somehow my name had gotten out in the medical community, and calls like that one came more and more frequently. At that time a decade ago, nutrition was not on the lips of the average American physician. That fact is changing, of course, but even today you have to choose doctors carefully if you care about using natural remedies where possible, instead of relying entirely on drugs.

Initially I began my nutritional studies purely as a means of helping my own body. I had become positively, vitally, actively committed to doing everything possible not only to heal my cancer, but to go even beyond that. I wanted to attain the best health status possible for myself.

After three years of study, trials and life changes, at age fifty, three years after my mastectomy, I had regained the weight I lost during Charlene's final battles. Now I looked the picture of health.

Meanwhile, nutrition was becoming a hot topic across America. Women's groups and local television shows, eager to feature programs on nutrition and supplements, began inviting me to speak on the subject. By now my name had become linked with the nutrition topic, so the invitations flowed in. Best of all, my energy was increasing. I needed extra energy. My workdays began early and usually ended late.

New Purpose

I did not consider myself an authority on nutrition or anything else. Still, my phone was ringing a dozen times a day with calls from professionals and lay people who wanted information or, many times, advice.

"We don't believe in this. We don't know anything about it," doctors would begin once we were connected by telephone.

"We're not saying that vitamins, nutrients or any of this nutritional or alternative stuff is any good, but you look pretty good. You have survived cancer, and you look pretty good. Would you mind talking to Mrs. Jones, or would you mind telling me what you do? Or could I have this patient call you?"

Overnight, it seemed, people were telling people, and doctors were telling their patients, to phone me. People, people, people!

So my secretary and I tackled all the inquiries, beginning at eight o'clock in the morning and often continuing into the evening hours. People were calling me from everywhere, not wanting information so much as they hungered to hear my experience of surviving cancer. Back then the general knowledge did not exist. People learned by asking, "What is your experience as a nutritionist?"

Of course, I really was not a nutritionist. I had no formal training for that role. All I could say was, "I have lived the life. I have had the disease. I had to experience that in order to begin taking proper care of my body." All I could share was what had happened in my life—cancer was my experience.

Dee Simmons does not prescribe. I will tell anyone anything I know about a supplement or the function of various vitamins, minerals or other dietary elements. But I will not prescribe for you!

My training? That was largely gleaned from some of the world's finest experts on nutrition and wellness. I would contact those world-class nutritionists, usually by telephone, and simply ask to consult with them. Often I flew to distant cities to meet with a busy physician or an expert researcher who was willing to answer my questions and guide me toward further research.

This was cutting-edge stuff. I often marveled that many of the greatest people are the most generous about imparting what they know. God allowed many wonderful doors to open wide for me. Whenever I asked I was able to learn about the results of the latest studies in specific areas and what implications the studies suggested to the career scientists who conducted them. Looking back, I feel amazed at how boldly I approached some of the most eminent people in the nutrition field.

Obviously these experts must have realized that this cancer survivor had an intense, very serious interest in learning more about the natural elements so fundamental to human health. Indeed, very early I set a goal to learn one new fact about nutrition every single day.

Time of Transition

This transition period in my life proved highly challenging. At the time our leases had not yet expired, and I still had my fashion showrooms and a staff of ten talented and loyal people.

Placing my fashion showrooms entirely in the hands of my staff members, I turned to the job and privilege of working at my new calling. The demanding pace of what I chose to do was my best antidote to my heartbreak over Charlene's death—or so I thought.

The truth was, I had suffered that grief down inside. There it stayed as I attempted to transcend that hurtful event through serving others like Charlene and me. I wanted so much to make a difference in other people's lives.

Underneath, however, the torment of not knowing why I had to lose my irreplaceable friend was never far from my conscious thinking. This went beyond pain and loss. It spoke to our almost uncanny similarities, our "sisterhood" and "twinship," and even the fact that we had suffered the same cancer experiences only one month apart.

Having said all that brings me to the very edge of the mental precipice I can't bear to look into. Charlene and I had identical diagnoses and identical procedures . . . so, OK . . . if it happened to Charlene, it's going to happen to me. Besides, I'm not worthy to

97

live, if Charlene had not been spared. She was such a wonderful person.

Grief is not rational. My mind endlessly returned to the thoughts I just described. But I never dealt with those thoughts. Instead, I let fear—deep-seated, immovable, nauseating, white-knuckle fear—invade my heart and spirit.

Meanwhile, I sat at my desk seven days a week, all day long, helping people. I talked to cancer patients, some very sick, others who were dying and others still shocked by their recent cancer prognosis.

Away from that desk, I'm at the hospital with a cancer patient. Or I'm in a waiting room with a cancer patient, waiting for the family or waiting for the doctor to come out and tell us what he found.

Realize, most everyone who telephones me is sick—most everyone! The calls never stop coming, and they are so important to me. Soon I no longer had time for most of my friends. I certainly could not spare time for parties, functions or travel—the lifestyle I had previously enjoyed. I was developing new friendships instead, relating to people all over the world whom I didn't even know. Hearing their stories all day long, absorbing their fears and making them my own. They were calling to ask, "How can I get well?" I had a burning desire in my heart to somehow find answers for their questions—and my own.

In the fashion world, I had been fearless. In this new world, one of such burning importance to me, I often felt riddled with guilt over having survived Charlene and fear-struck over any small bruise, bump or swelling on my body.

God clearly had set my feet on a new path. I felt certain of this. Meanwhile, His enemy saw fit to attack me and try to knock me off my course. The tool he used, of course, was fear. I determined not to allow him to stop me.

The Promise

You and I want to know about those who have cancer and live. More and more people do live, and if they take charge of their lives they have a great chance to continue living. These success stories keep us going.

Way back in the beginning when I had that little office in my home, I made God a promise. Understanding how much a cancer patient can hurt, and how much some simply need a listening ear, I promised God that I would never, ever, turn down a cancer patient who needed to talk to me. Even today, busy as my hectic schedule becomes traveling around the country, ministering, appearing on television . . . my top priority is the list of cancer patients I am to telephone.

Late one night, however, I nearly broke my promise to God. I had had three exhausting telephone conferences earlier that day. I was already in bed when the telephone rang very insistently, and I "just knew" it would be a cancer patient calling from some faraway city where the evening still was young.

Actually, I was sound asleep, but I could hear the telephone ringing and ringing. I dreaded the idea of forcing myself awake. I lay there ardently hoping that Glenn would answer and tell whoever was there that I was sleeping. But instead, Glenn came into my bed, saying, "Honey, there's another cancer patient on the phone."

"Glenn, I just can't do it tonight," I told my husband. "I'm simply too tired. You'll have to tell them that I'll have to call them back."

Never will I forget his response. He looked down at me with all the kindness and compassion in the world on his face.

"Dee, you have to do it," he gently reminded me. "You made God a promise. You have to do it."

I got out of that bed, walked into my study and picked up the telephone. And when I began speaking to that person who was hurting, who was so in need, who just needed that one little word of encouragement to hope again, something happened. The anointing came over me, and a refreshing came over my weary body. When I finished with that person I felt as though I'd had an eight-hour sleep. God put a hedge of protection around me. He prevented me from breaking my promise to Him.

Decide to Live

David the psalmist wrote: "I shall not die but live, and shall declare the works and recount the illustrious acts of the Lord" (Ps. 118:17).

Any of us who deal with cancer can take a lesson from that bold scripture: "I shall not die but live." Notice that David does not mention murderous enemies, wild animals, advancing armies or anything else. David kept his eyes on what he wanted. He ignored every obstacle and simply focused on the goodness of God.

We can do the same. When I decided to take charge over my health, the idea was to survive. I wanted to save my physical life. I researched, studied and did all in my power to reestablish my good health.

God certainly has honored my basic intention, but He had far more in His plan for me than I could have dreamed. He knew that the results of my search would benefit not just me, but thousands of other people like me . . . an army of the sick and broken.

I believe our decision to live becomes a first step. After that, God leads us to step two, step three and so on, as we climb closer toward Him.

Deciding to live, I notice, always changes people's priorities. I know mine took a one-hundred-eighty-degree turn. Before cancer, I never could have dreamed that I would willingly replace my enviable lifestyle with days devoted to the sick and dying. I would have told you that I had everything I could want and didn't desire any changes. My life seemed nearly perfect in most ways. I could not have imagined that it would change into something far more satisfying and life giving. Also, I had little or no idea of how much restoration can happen . . . once we start giving away those same blessings God first gave us.

It's fascinating to see how even those with terminal cancer can bless themselves and others by deciding to live—and notice, no one has asked any of us, "How long?" Deciding to live means deciding to make each day of one's life more purposeful and worry free.

God wants us to live fully and abundantly. Ironically, more than one cancer patient has stated that only a cancer experience could have resulted in his deciding to live. Of course, God does not give us cancer. But He does give us the victory once we decide we will not die, but live.

The Price

My husband says, "I seldom see you without a Bible or a nutrition book in your hand." He is right, but those are the books I now enjoy. God has totally changed my priorities.

Reading about nutrition is one of my favorite things to do. Before I go to bed each night, my personal goal requires me to learn a new nutrition fact—one a day, like a vitamin pill. You say, "How do you learn?" Well, I subscribe to every health newsletter I can find and, of course, produce my own newsletter. I read everything I can on my subject of choice. God has been so gracious to allow me to meet some of the world's leading authorities in the nutrition field. Many of these people have become my friends.

But at the same time, I realize I must take care of

myself. When I have counseled with cancer patients during the day, often I retire early, then find myself waking up in the very early hours of the morning. Sometimes God wakes me up, and I just lie there and weep and weep. He has given me a burden for those who suffer or are needy.

Like any other cancer patient, I know what it's like to walk through the valley of the shadow of death. And I walk, along with those people, from the time they are diagnosed until the day of their final victory. If I pay a price in terms of physical energy and time and effort spent, the ultimate rewards far exceed anything I could expend. If God has allowed me to see the valley of the shadow of death, he also has allowed me to see priceless victories and blessings.

He will do the same for you.

Blessings

Today I have thousands upon thousands of friends. I enjoy more friends than ever before in my life, because I give them hope. Sometimes, in fact, God allows me to point them to something of eternal value: a personal relationship with God through faith in Jesus Christ.

People telephone me from many parts of the globe. Many do not know God personally. Some do not believe in God, and I do not try to ram my beliefs down their throats. But always, whether in a telephone or personal conversation, I say, "Remember one thing. There is hope. There is a Great Physician. Would you allow me to pray with you?"

Never has any person refused. As I pray, God always gives me the words, and I can hear the person at the other end of the telephone line sobbing with a broken heart. God continually blesses me with knowing that He would have me minister to their soul, their emotions, their physical selves—everything at the same time.

We live in a fallen and imperfect world. Only One Person is perfect. But in my own imperfect life, I can see how often God redeems our mistakes, words, thoughts and deeds. I believe He allowed me to suffer pain so I could later identify with others who suffer.

"I hurt."

"I lost my best friend."

"I have fear."

I know that our God walks with us through the fire of sickness and disease. And when we come safely to the other side of our personal affliction, He stays by our side. By then most of us will have discovered a new power and purpose in our lives. This is the abundant life He yearns to give us.

Nine

Ultimate Victory

MOTHER AND I MIGHT BE BEST friends, but our time together had become more and more limited. With our houses just eight blocks apart, we'd usually visit every day and telephone one another a couple of times. This was getting harder and harder to do. My schedule was unbelievable. Hers was not much better. Mother believed that when God needed hands and feet, hers were the only ones He had to use. She loved to serve others.

In the church where I grew

up, and where Mother and Daddy worshiped and served all my life, in 1988 honored my mother as "Mother of the Year." That was fitting, I thought. You couldn't count all the people who "adopted" her as their surrogate mother. She was interested in everyone. She was a "prayer warrior" who prayed for many people consistently and repeatedly. She really involved herself with people.

So in July 1992, as we prepared for our annual vacation on the island of Maui, I knew Mother, Daddy, Glenn and I all needed a good rest. There could be no better place for it. In fact, it had become such a favorite getaway, especially for Mother, that Glenn bought a condominium there for our family.

That year, however, Mother said she really didn't want to go. She felt extra tired, and her back hurt. "No wonder you feel tired," I chided her. "Your back hurts because you have quit exercising. I want you to come to Maui and get a good rest. You'll have a wonderful time and feel good. You don't have to do a thing but feed the cats."

Her cats had become a big joke between us. We stayed in a high-stilted house facing the ocean. Hordes of island cats roamed under the houses. There were signs everywhere forbidding us to feed them, but she paid no attention. At restaurants she'd scan the menu, saying, "Let's see. I wonder what the cats would like." We kidded her that her every meal had to be built around the best leftovers she could take home to the cats.

Back in Texas, Mother was known for being particular about food. She would not eat fat, use salt or drink coffee. I have seen her wash vegetables someone else prepared, removing all the salt before she would eat them. She stayed tiny and slim. She never used nutritional supplements, but she ate right.

My mother also kept a healthy-minded attitude toward our family's health. True, I had all those gynecological problems and also had asthma all my life, but except for those maladies I was healthy. None of us got anything out of staying in bed or talking about our ailments. And even when I had breast cancer, Mother never seemed all that perturbed. Her attitude was, "We know you will survive this thing. You will be just fine."

So I wasn't going to let her stay home from our vacation because she felt tired. I persuaded her to go, and we all went. Once we got to Maui for our "rest," however, it turned out to be anything but. Mother mostly stayed in her bedroom with a heating pad on her sore back. She and I didn't have our usual fun times, our special lunches and good conversations. Mostly we chatted in her room. "You know, Diane, my stomach is swollen," she remarked one day.

Then Glenn came down with a viral infection that made him feel miserable. The doctor prescribed antibiotics as his fever climbed higher and higher. Glenn, who always thinks of others, knew he was contagious and insisted on renting a separate apartment for himself so he would not infect the rest of us.

Nobody had a great time that year. Between Mother's heating pad and Glenn's antibiotics, we stayed pretty much housebound. The cats got little pampering. It was a lousy vacation.

The first ten days after our return home were not much better. Glenn continued to hack and cough. I instructed Mother to see her doctor. And meanwhile, I had come home to a desk overflowing with messages, memos and things that needed my attention. For me, it was catch-up time. Consequently, it was days before I had so much as a real telephone chat with my mother.

That was highly unusual. For one thing, my husband and I frequently dine out in the evenings. Often we'd call Mother and Daddy and take them out for a fabulous meal. There were a couple of reasons why we always went out. For one thing, Glenn and I love discovering fancy new restaurants. Beyond that, Glenn said he wanted to get me away from all the telephones and have me to himself.

"You have seventeen telephones in the house, and they are always ringing," he told me. "We have four lines, and all of them stay busy. I need to get you away from all those ringing telephones."

During those ten days or so, however, we didn't get far from the telephones, and I didn't visit my mother. When we finally talked, she told me her doctor had prescribed antibiotics.

"He thinks I picked up whatever Glenn had," she told me. I felt uneasy with that explanation. After all, she had been complaining about not feeling well even before we left for Hawaii, I recalled. A few days later, I quizzed her again.

"Mother, do you still feel sick?"

"Yes, I still don't feel good, honey. I'm going back to the doctor."

She returned for another doctor's visit, and I didn't think much about it. Afterward I called to check on her, and she said, "They asked me a funny question today at the doctor's office."

"What did they ask you?"

"They asked me if anyone in my family ever had cancer. I said, 'Well, my daughter had breast cancer.' And they said, 'Well, you don't have cancer, Mrs. Gee. But while you are here, let's go ahead and run some other tests. We want to do a liver scan.'"

My blood ran cold. "A liver scan?" I asked her. "Are you sure it was a liver scan? Mother, why would they do that? That doesn't make any sense. They have you on an antibiotic because you don't feel good and may have a chest infection. So they ran a liver scan?"

"I think so," Mother told me. "It was a scan."

"When do you go in and get the results?"

"Thursday morning at nine o'clock," she said.

That Tuesday evening I felt real disbelief as I hung up the telephone. Turning to Glenn, I asked, "Why does it make sense to run a liver scan on my mother?

Why would they do something like that?"

"I don't know," he said.

"It's stupid," I told him.

That unanswered question hovered over me all Tuesday night and all day Wednesday. I thought, *I'll not even tell Mother, but I'm going to show up at that doctor's office on Thursday morning when they go over the results of all those tests.*

Early Thursday morning Glenn asked his usual question: "What are you going to do today?"

"I thought I'd meet Mother at her doctor's office," I said in passing, as I headed out the door and got in my red Jeep. I drove out to Plano and arrived just in time. Mother and Daddy were driving up at the same time I did. As we pulled up simultaneously, I glanced to my right and saw Glenn pulling in next to me. I thought, *What in the world?*

My husband is the most sensitive and caring man in all the world. I'll never forget my mental picture of our three cars—Daddy's, mine and Glenn's—pulling into those parking places together and parking side by side.

Then came the real shock. As Mother gets out of her car, I see she is wearing a bathrobe! People who know me know I don't go anywhere, even the grocery store, unless everything looks perfect. Every hair, every bit of makeup, everything matching . . . I don't wear casual. I'm not a casual person, and I get that from my mother.

My mother dressed. Everything matched. Everything had to be coordinated—the shoes, blouse, jewelry, everything. She was dainty, fastidious and did everything to perfection. And now she is arriving at the doctor's office in her robe!

I felt embarrassed. I couldn't believe my mother would appear in public in her robe. What was she doing? I felt almost irritated that this woman who had never done such a thing in her life was suddenly appearing at a doctor's office dressed that way. Usually mother got up early in the morning and immediately made herself beautiful.

"Mother! Why do you have on your robe?" I called out.

"Well, honey, I just didn't feel like dressing," she replied.

Once seated in the doctor's office, however, things seemed somewhat more normal. Mother's doctor seemed cheerful and positive as he ran through her test results. "Your blood work looks terrific," he assured her, "and this is great, and that is great . . ." I was beginning to think Mother was in such excellent condition she could run a marathon.

"However," the doctor concluded, "the scan we did showed a spot on your pancreas." At that I literally leaped up, leaned across the desk and grabbed the doctor's coat.

"What do you mean, 'a spot on her pancreas'?" I asked. I knew about "spots." I also knew about the pancreas. I did not want my mother to have any spot on her pancreas.

"There's just this little suspicious spot," he said.

"Doctor! Tell me what you mean," I implored. "You are talking to a cancer survivor. You are talking to someone who works with cancer patients every day of her life. I know about spots. Explain this spot to me!"

Unruffled, my mother's doctor informed us in a quiet, low-key voice, that we were to visit a "Doctor Smith" to whom he was referring my mother. Dr. Smith would explain the situation to us. Turning to my mother, he added, "Mrs. Gee, he will have to do a little surgery. He has to go in there and look at that spot."

"I can't do that right now," Mother answered. "I'm too tired and weak. I'll have to wait a few weeks before we can do surgery."

"No, Mrs. Gee, you have to do it now," he told her. "Go see Dr. Smith, and let him explain it to you."

I stood up, too numb to feel anything, and got directions to Dr. Smith's office, some three miles down the road. I felt totally, totally numb. We got in our respective cars, and the moment I headed my jeep down the road I picked up my telephone and called Dr. George Peters on his private beeper. I always knew I could reach him anywhere. Even if he were operating, they would put the phone on his ear, and he would advise me.

"Dr. Peters is performing surgery," they told me.

"Tell him this is Dee," I somehow managed to get out.

Immediately George Peters answered. When he heard my weeping, my incoherent message, at first he thought I had been in an automobile accident. "The doctor just told my mother she has a spot on her pancreas, and now we're in the car and on the way to see this Dr. Smith," I told him.

"What do you mean, Dr. Smith?" he asked. "What are you talking about, Dee?" By now I was crying so hysterically I could hardly drive. Dr. Peters took over the conversation.

"Go ahead and see Dr. Smith," he ordered. "Then I will call some doctors together, and you be here in an hour."

A Medical Godsend

Dr. Smith, as I'm calling him, turned out to be the most precious Christian you'd ever want to meet. A gentleman, a surgeon, he led us into a small room where he could see my mother's x-ray scans. Mother sat on the edge of an examining table. The rest of us were standing, me leaning against a wall.

"Mrs. Gee, you have cancer," Dr. Smith gently informed her. "You have one of the very worst stages of pancreatic cancer. It would be more helpful if the cancer were on the tip of the pancreas, but yours is in the center of the organ. We can't do anything about this. You will not survive."

There is no way in the world to describe my feelings. Leaning against that wall, trying not to faint or slide to the floor, not wanting to absorb the unthinkable news we had just received . . .

But my mother remained totally at ease. "You have the very worst kind of pancreatic cancer," her doctor repeated, wanting to make sure Mother understood. "You are not going to live."

"OK, Dr. Smith," she responded in her usual natural, friendly way. "How long do you think I will live?"

"Maybe three months," he told her.

"Maybe *six* months," he amended, unconvincingly.

A Glorious Light

It is important to tell what happened next. Events of the next several minutes in that ordinary little medical office helped carry us through the weeks ahead and transformed my life forever.

"Dr. Smith, that's OK," Mother reassured him. You could see her concern that he had to convey such painful news. Then the doctor slowly stepped back, a look of awe on his face, as the room literally lit up like a bright light.

Everything became gloriously illuminated. It became so bright in that little office that you could hardly bear to look. "Mrs. Gee! I can't believe what I see on your countenance," Dr. Smith breathed, sounding amazed and awed.

"I just told you that you are going to die. Now I see

this glow . . . like a halo around your head!"

Time seemed to stand still as my mother's voice sounded through all that gleaming light. She sounded so calm, so normal, so like my mother always sounded. "Don't you understand, Dr. Smith? I am a Christian. I know I am going home to be with Jesus. I have run my race. Now I am going to get my reward."

Her voice, her words, sounded like a benediction. We all stood motionless as her thoughts poured into the room like a prayer. "I love water, Dr. Smith, and the Bible talks about the little streams . . . I love little birds and I'll be able to sit beside those streams and enjoy the waters and the little birds.

"In heaven there are so many beautiful things I love . . . birds, flowers . . . so much goodness and beauty. Please don't worry about it. The only thing you may have to help me with is my husband and my daughter. My daughter may not handle this very well, Dr. Smith, and she's the one I worry about.

"Just pray for Diane. Don't pray for me. And pray for my husband."

We stood there, all of us, in total shock and speechless. And then, in a moment, we were back to a world of practicalities. "Mrs. Gee, we have to put you in the hospital," Dr. Smith said. "We must do exploratory surgery right away. We also must drain off some fluid that is building up in your body."

Driving on Central Expressway toward Baylor Hospital, our three cars in cavalcade, I still could not believe what I had heard. *Maybe Dr. Smith can't help my mother, but Dr. Peters has other famous doctors waiting for us*, I thought. *They are supposed to be the best in the world. They will be able to do something to save my mother.*

Dr. Peters and a distinguished cancer surgeon were waiting for us. I was called into his office before our consultation started. The surgeon lit up my mother's x-ray and said, "Dee, Dr. Smith was right. Your mother has terminal cancer."

"How long will she live?" I asked.

"She may live three months. She could live six months. I can refer you to other oncologists, but I know she cannot live."

"I know about pancreatic cancer," I told him. "I will not put my mother through chemotherapy, which cannot save her life." He looked at me, his face full of compassion, and simply nodded. He understood.

Again, my mother, father and husband heard the news.

"Oh, that's OK," Mother said, trying to reassure us. Her smile said this was the best news she had received in her life. I could not believe her reaction.

Soon our three cars pulled into the driveway of our house. Silently, we walked into the den. My mother, still in her robe, suddenly decided to take charge.

"I'm hungry!" she announced. "Glenn, would you please go out and get me a hamburger? I want the biggest, greasiest hamburger you can find. Get me a *big* hamburger!" This is my mother, the woman who didn't drink coffee or eat fats . . . demanding a *hamburger*.

Anger

My daddy, mother and I were alone now. We had privacy for the first time all day. I fell to the floor and had a temper tantrum like you wouldn't believe. I was so mad at God. I felt so *angry*.

Here I was, supposedly a grown woman, kicking, screaming and beating my fists on the floor. I was having a tantrum. "God! How can You do this to my mother?

"When my mother prays, things happen. She has a hotline to heaven . . . to You. How can You take this woman's life? A woman who ministers, who gives her life to everyone?

"My mother never turns anyone away. She prays for everyone. And now You are going to take her? How can You be that cruel? If You wanted to take someone with cancer, why not me? Why would You take my mother?"

I felt so angry that He would consider taking my mother. I had not served the Lord all my life. I had backslidden. I had sinned. But here was my mother, so perfect in my eyes and in the eyes of so many others, so if it had to be somebody, why not me?

As I screamed, sobbed and said all these things, my mother walked over and placed her arms around me. "Honey, don't you understand?" she asked. "It's OK. Mother is just going on to heaven ahead of you. I get to be up there with Jesus."

As my sobs subsided, she continued in a quiet, happy way, "This just means I will be passing my mantle on to you. If my life and what I have lived and my testimony are to mean anything at all, it will be your responsibility to carry these things forward."

Responsibility

At that moment, it hit me. My mother is handing these things over to me. This mother who always had been so spiritually centered, the strong leader, the stable influence, the glue that kept us all together.

Now my mother is telling me this would be my responsibility. She was asking me to make that sort of commitment, and I know how unworthy I am.

Mother ate the hamburger Glenn brought her and soon went home. She seemed fine, but I was in shock—a prelude to the feelings of utter devastation I felt for days.

Dr. Smith performed surgery on Mother just days later. Afterward, he emerged with more bad news. Most of her internal organs had been invaded, he told us. Again, I felt devastated, yet once again my mother came out of the recovery room smiling.

"Oh, that's OK," she said, when she learned the truth. We took her home to recuperate, and I would stay with her in the daytime. My sister, Sandra, soon came for a good visit, and our brother, James, who lived nearby, popped in at least once a day.

Meanwhile Mother, too weak to get out of bed,

started planning her future. I became her "gofer" as she sorted through her belongings and assigned them to one person or another. "I want D'Andra to have my fur coats and these diamond rings," she announced cheerfully. She had me tagging everything she especially liked, and she enjoyed choosing what went to whom. One day I realized that she and I were having real quality time together, actually far better visits and conversations than we got to have a few weeks earlier in Maui.

Mother's condition deteriorated rapidly, however. From the day of her diagnosis, she lived only four weeks and three days . . . a period in which I desperately savored every visit and hoarded every word she spoke.

Mother always had been a planner, and I inherited that. Now she got me to help plan her "graduation" ceremony. She knew exactly what she wanted to wear—a pink silk dress of mine she had always liked. "Also," she instructed, "I want a beautiful white handkerchief in my hand." I smiled at that. Mother loved dainty handkerchiefs because Mother always cried. She was so compassionate. If you told her your story, she'd start crying, and then she'd pray with you.

So she always had a white hanky nearby, and she liked lacey ones. She collected white hankies with lace. I had just received a beautiful white handkerchief from Europe, so I said, "OK, Mother, here's the white handkerchief." We even found a little bird, preserved through taxidermy, that we placed in her casket. She wanted that.

As the time drew nearer, Mother would say, "Now I want to plan . . ." She planned her entire service to the last detail. She had written hundreds of poems, and she chose one for the printed program.

"Mother, would you like for me to speak at your memorial service?" I asked one day.

"Honey, yes I would, but you won't be able to," she said. "You'll get too upset, too brokenhearted."

"No, Mother, somehow God will give me the strength. He will give me what I need to do this. I will be able to do it," I promised.

"There are two things I want you to say then, honey," she responded. "First, it's so important that you present the plan of salvation. Some people who come may not know the Lord. And the other thing is, please thank everyone for all they have done for me, but most of all, for loving me. That's real important."

Of course, I promised to do everything Mother asked. Our planning sessions were not all that painful, really. They were sweet. In fact, those weeks held some of the best times we'd ever known together. But the truth is, even as I agreed to all she asked, the reality of Mother's situation still had not yet come home to me. I still believed God would miraculously heal my mother.

One afternoon just after Mother's surgery I received a telephone call from Lindsay Roberts, wife of Richard Roberts and daughter-in-law of evangelist Oral Roberts. I had met Lindsay only once before, but she was calling to say she had learned about mother and wanted to drive to Dallas and pray for her.

"Richard and I will be taping tonight," she told me, "but we'll come right after that." That meant Richard and Lindsay arrived in Dallas at 3 A.M., checked into a hotel and met with us in Mother's hospital room the next day. After praying with Mother and comforting her, they had dinner with Glenn and me before driving back home to Oklahoma City. What friends they are!

Two weeks later, Mother was failing fast. I phoned Lindsay with a big request. A world-famous evangelist was coming to Dallas for a huge crusade. I wanted to take Mother there for prayer. "Can you help us with this, Lindsay?" I appealed.

"I'll take care of it," Lindsay Roberts promised. Minutes later she called back. "I'll fly down, and we'll take your mother through a back entrance. I'll go with you. It's all arranged for her."

By now Mother was too weak to walk. We had help at night and wonderful home hospice care during the day. So mother attended the crusade in a wheelchair. When the healing service began, we took her on stage—Lindsay Roberts, my dad and I, my brother, James, and Glenn. Immediately after Mother received prayer, we took her right home.

Later Daddy told me that on the way home God spoke to him and told him it was Mother's time to go. That same night, however, I continued to cling to hope. Sometimes, staying with her, I'd beg, "Mother, please write me one more thing—just one more note." She had given me hundreds over the years, but I still longed to have just one more.

"Honey, I'm just too tired," she would say. "Mother can't write anything else."

One night I knelt beside her bed and looked into her face. I began to cry. "Mother, please don't die. Aren't you afraid to die? Aren't you? Mother, please tell me." I thought she had such power, such a voice in God's ear, that she could still say, "OK, God, I have decided not to die." I believed He would listen.

"Oh honey, I'm not afraid to die," my mother answered. No matter how many times I'd lament that way, no matter how much I wept, her answers never varied.

"Honey, Mother is just going on ahead of you. I will be with the Lord, but I am placing my mantle on you."

Divine Mantle

Those early mornings, I would get out and walk, think and pray, "Dear God, please let me sense Your presence and blessing. Please give me what You want me to say when my mother goes home to be with You. Help me to celebrate my mother's life. Help me to speak without crying." Over and over I prayed that. I was so scared I could not do those things.

Mother took care to tell me several things she wanted me to remember. "You will have a ministry," she said. "You will help hundreds and thousands of cancer patients with the knowledge God has given you. You must not give up your ministry call to help others.

"What you know can't help Mother, but you must continue going on from here," she told me. "You will help other mothers. Above all, remember your promise to God. Promise me you will keep that promise."

"I will, Mother."

On September 21, 1992, my mother finished her race. That beautiful autumn day, she slipped into a final coma. Several of our closest family members and friends gathered around her bedside—Daddy and my brother, Glenn and me, D'Andra, her pastor and his wife, Mike Tadlock and his wife Rogene, who are two of Mother's very special "kids," my best friend, Marian Barnes, who has stood with me during so many tough times, and our friends Terry and Ruthie Smith.

"Precious (important and no light matter) in the sight of the Lord is the death of His saints—His loving ones)" (Ps. 116:15). Watching my mother slip from this life into the next somewhere around three that afternoon, I thought it was like a child who gently fell asleep.

How easy it seemed to be, after all. Looking down at Mother's tranquil face, I saw so many evidences of God's daily love and mercy. Her disease had progressed swiftly. She had had little pain. She had no fear. She was comatose only during her final two or three hours. She was able to be at home.

Here she rested, surrounded by those who loved her dearly. How precious in our sight she was, as well as in the sight of the Lord!

Some one thousand friends crowded into Gospel Lighthouse Church on the afternoon of Saturday, September 23, 1992, to celebrate the life of Mary Maxine McCoy Gee, who for fifty-three years had been the wife of Bill Gee. During that half-century, Mickie Gee had mothered, mentored, motivated and lifted up in prayer countless individuals. What a testimony to what God can do through the life of one "average housewife!"

Then I was speaking to that huge crowd, telling them about my angel mother. I had absolutely no fear! Instead, I sensed God's presence helping me. The words flowed, words that made people laugh and cry. Afterward many obtained tapes of the service. As Mother had asked, I told people how they could have peace with God through a personal relationship with Jesus Christ.

Peaceful Death

Mother approached her illness and death as a strong Christian. She possessed an overcoming faith. Her spirit remained serene as she accepted each day's challenges.

This was death, which I had so feared and fought against for Mother, Charlene and myself. *I hate cancer,* I thought for the millionth time.

124

But God was showing me that Mother, during her final weeks, had shown all of us how to *live*. She lived then, and she lives now, I realized. We did not lose her. We know exactly where she is.

"What was that scripture she gave me?" I asked myself. Then I remembered her telling me something I had not known. She had come to see me in the hospital when I was so sick following my cancer surgery.

"I pushed open that massive door of the Roberts Building," she began. "I said, 'O God, please don't take my daughter's life!' With that He spoke to me and gave me a scripture: 'I shall not die, but live, and shall declare the works and recount the illustrious acts of the Lord' (Ps. 118:17).

"That was the day God gave me assurance in my heart that you would live," she told me. "Do you know why?

"One reason is the scripture that says, 'Regard (treat with honor, due obedience, and courtesy) your father and mother, that your days may be long in the land the Lord your God gives you' (Exod. 20:12). Lots of times you were not the perfect child. Often you went back into the world. But, honey, you always honored your father and mother. And your heavenly Father always keeps His promise."

So I accepted that final word from my mother—I shall not die, but live. May His will be done in my life and in yours.

125

Ten

An Amazing Year

JUST TWO MONTHS FOLLOWING my mother's death, a newly formed nutrition company came to me with the offer of becoming its corporate chairman and spokesperson. It seemed like an ideal opportunity. I had by no means completed my grieving process, but I mistakenly believed that plunging myself into this worthwhile new endeavor would help.

Months of exhausting travel, platform speaking and television appearances followed. I was

126

working eighteen-hour days, pouring myself into the mission and vision God had given me. The desire to help other people became a burning passion in my heart. As Mother had said, my knowledge couldn't help her, but I dreamed of helping others like her.

So I threw myself into this with all the indescribable drive I have and with all the passion and love to help people get well. Besides talking with cancer patients all day, as I had done before, I also traveled, going into an office and making time for increasing numbers of television shows.

Nutrition and alternative medicine were now part of the general public's vocabulary, and I had done my part to bring that about. Because of my cancer experience, I had moved out considerably ahead of the general trend, and by now people recognized my name, my face and, to a large extent, my message.

I worked for that company for just over twelve months, when an unexpected thing happened. God gave me a scripture: "Be still, and know (recognize and understand) that I am God" (Ps. 46:10).

God made me understand that I was to pull back. I clearly knew I was to leave that company and wait on Him. "You are to do nothing," He instructed me. "Be still. I have a plan for you. I want you to stop everything you are doing and wait."

That was that. I obeyed Him.

January came, and February, and suddenly I was invited to be interviewed for a position as talk show host for a major new television show on health-related issues. I flew back from that meeting tremendously excited. It seemed they thought I was perfect for the assignment. It would be a daily show . . . all health related . . . what could be more perfect?

In March, God spoke to me again. "I told you to be still. You are not to do this. Wait on Me." For the second time in my life, I got mad at God.

"Are You ever going to use me?" I demanded of Him. "I have studied. I have traveled. I have ministered to people. Why don't You want me to do this?"

There was no answer. By now I felt thoroughly confused, because several nutrition companies came to me, asking me to become their spokesperson. Each time I was tempted. The role suits me, because I believe so passionately that we must motivate people to improve their health habits.

Months passed, and still God did not reveal His plan for me. Meanwhile, I argued with Him often, because so many offers were coming to me. God kept saying, "Be still. Be still. Be still."

During those months of waiting as I tried to still my impatient self and stop the arguments between the human and the Divine, tests of integrity were taking place. Slowly I began to realize that none of these nutrition company positions could have been right for me.

Every company I talked with had good products. Their complete product line typically had several really superior products, while others in the line would be less good. None of the lines was totally consistent. "The consumer doesn't know," one man explained. "Why use high-priced ingredients when the consumer simply doesn't know the difference?"

That bothered me a lot. I believed each product should possess equal integrity—the best of the best. Silently I was beginning to understand some fundamental things about myself and my beliefs about excellent nutrition products. For example, I believed:

- Cost should never prohibit the use of top-quality ingredients.
- Each item in a product line should meet highest quality standards.
- Cleanliness and pharmaceutical-level laboratory standards are essential.

The truth was, my standards were much higher than some people's. I simply could not pretend that anything less than the purest and the best could be acceptable. After all, real integrity demands no less.

By now it had been four years since my mother died. "I know what you are supposed to do," Glenn said.

My husband had come in from work and found me at my desk. Now he looked down at me with a serious expression on his face that I couldn't quite read.

"I know what you are supposed to do," he repeated. "What?"

I looked up in surprise. Glenn never says things like

that. I always make my own decisions. But I could tell he was ready to spring something big. Also, I could tell he felt sure he was right about whatever it was.

"Honey, the only way you are going to be happy," he continued, "and be able to go on helping others is to start your own nutrition company."

For once, I was totally speechless. The idea had come from way out in left field. It was something I never would have thought.

I hardly knew how to reply. I was flabbergasted!

"However, I don't really want you to do that," Glenn began back-pedaling. "It would be a heavy responsibility for you, with long hours and hard work, and I know you'd throw yourself into it with everything you've got.

"So if you won't do it . . ." By now he had turned around and begun to walk away. That's when I cut in.

"Oh, good! That's great. Glenn! That's a great idea. I hadn't thought of that. I never would have thought of it."

"If you decide not to do it," he went on, "I'll give you something I've never given you before." He walked out of the room. When he returned he handed me a blank check. "Take this check. I have signed it. If you decide not to start a nutrition company, you can fill out this check for any amount you want."

I felt shocked. Glenn was dead serious. I had no idea what was going on. So I sat there with the check in my hand, stupified by everything that was unfolding. Glenn is the most responsible man in the world. He is an extremely generous husband, but also highly responsible with the wealth God has entrusted to him. He does not play around with money. He uses it wisely.

Glenn placed his hand on mine and said, "You don't have to think about any of this right now. Just take this check, and you pray about it. If you decide not to start up your nutrition company, and if you'll stop doing some of the things you stay so busy with, then I'll retire and we will travel around the world and enjoy our remaining years. And you can keep the check.

"If you do decide to start your nutrition company, just return the check to me. Take a few days to decide if you need to."

That night I lay sleepless for a long time, my mind jumping with questions and thoughts. My husband is such an idea man. His mind is full of million-dollar ideas. Why would he find one with my name on it, then offer me all the money I could want not to take the idea and run with it?

It didn't make sense. So I lay in bed, quietly praying, until abruptly I began to weep. I had no idea why I was crying. My tears and prayers continued to flow for hours. I felt overwhelmed with weeping, until at last I saw light begin to creep across the morning sky, and my crying ceased.

After breakfast the next morning I went to Glenn's study where he has his morning devotions, with his check in my hand. I tore that check into piece after piece after piece and laid the pieces in a tiny pile on Glenn's desk.

"Glenn, I can't take this," I told him. "I just can't. I've got to do this. I don't have a choice. I can't take this check, honey. I made a promise to God that for the rest of my life I would reach out to others and make a difference. If I do not develop nutritional supplements, effective products on the cutting edge—who will do this and not compromise? I must offer hope and encouragement to others in a crisis."

So I just sat there, crying, saying, "Honey, I can't do it. I can't take your check." It broke my heart, because I saw how sincere my husband was and how he really wanted me to back away. Glenn never asked me not to do anything. He always allowed me to use my best judgment. But I knew the sacrifice he would make if I gave up the rest of my private life and made a commitment to have my own company.

"Dee Simmons, OK," Glenn said. "You have made your decision. But when you start up this company, remember two things. Remember the word *integrity*. Remember your name is Simmons. Don't ever embarrass that name. And remember, you will never compromise.

"When you establish your company, you make the best nutritional supplements and products in the world. Do not compromise. Do not ever come back to me when you have perfected a product and say, 'If I had a little more money, if I had a little more time, if I had a little more resources . . .' Because if you're going to do this, do it first class, the way our family has done everything. You make the best nutrition products this country has ever had!"

Integrity

My husband, in his godly wisdom, had guided me into the most far-reaching decision of my life. Later, when I asked him what he thought my decision would be, he just smiled. He knew very well that God had a calling on my life. He knew how seriously I respected that mission. And he also knew that no amount of money would sway me away from what I believed God wanted me to do.

What he didn't take into consideration, however, was that my love for him could have caused me to reconsider. Glenn believed in the integrity of my commitment to God. Glenn's challenge to me was meant to help test and firm up that commitment.

New Directions

The foundation of my new nutrition company rested on a solid Rock, I believed. God had led me to take charge over my body, my disciplines and my health. He had led me to counsel one-on-one with thousands of sick and dying people. And only God Himself could have empowered me to invest years of study and research on a subject many others then considered less than valid. The girl who skipped through school without studying? God had changed her into someone willing to read twelve-inch-high stacks of scientific reports and learn the properties of a host of vitamins, minerals and other nutritional elements.

For the past two or three years I had experimented with vitamin combinations for my own use. Now I would have highly trained chemists and other specialists in the world's finest laboratories who would oversee the creation and production of my life-enhancing new products.

None of this had happened suddenly, I now realized. Step by step, God had led me, and often Glenn as well, to this point. Surely, then, He meant to establish this new business upon the most solid of foundations. Initial planning took place around our kitchen table. I had faith in the level of nutrition expertise I had acquired so far, and I felt confident that I could deal knowledgeably with the caliber of scientists, formulas, chemists and nutrition experts we would enlist.

The Journey Begins

We had accumulated a sizeable list of laboratories we needed to visit. As you know, America's number one industry is that of producing pharmaceutical drugs. Consequently, we have numerous first-class laboratories located across the country.

Now we began our trek from state to state, region to region, to choose the laboratory that would produce our products. I saw some wonderful facilities. I also saw others that came highly recommended, yet had insects crawling on the floors. I saw products being mixed in washtubs. And when the five o'clock whistle blew for workers to leave, they'd walk away leaving huge vats and mixers full of ingredients to sit uncovered overnight.

I could not believe some of the things we saw! However, we continued to travel and narrow our list of potential choices until we came to a very modern and businesslike facility in California. This was it, I decided. I would sign a contract with them and return to Dallas.

Fortunately, I took time to phone home first. I had had an urgent telephone message from a knowledgeable friend who strongly recommended our visiting a laboratory outside of San Diego. It was not that far away.

Why not? Glenn and I agreed. We changed our travel plans and headed to the lab. Its extremely busy owner managed to carve out a thirty-minute appointment time when he could see us.

The moment we drove up to that laboratory (I knew it was a well-known, impressive facility) something in me said, "This is it." Set amongst masses of beautiful flowers and sculptured design, the building itself looked elegant and magnificently established.

My heart beat faster as we opened the entrance door into a fine reception area. We were led into a gorgeous conference room, as nice as Glenn's office in Dallas.

Soon a doctor clothed from head to toe in white emerged from a security area. He was their chief chemist. Then Glenn and I, also swathed in white garments, were allowed into the laboratory area for our inspection tour. Immaculate! You could eat off those floors. State-of-the-art equipment. State-of-the-art technology. Isolation rooms where nothing was touched by human hands. White-gloved workers were everywhere, but sophisticated machines did every task imaginable.

In the mahogany-paneled library, shelves of scientific textbooks lined the walls. Researchers worked at computers or quietly consulted among themselves. So this was R & D—research and development—or at least a significant part of it!

The library opened onto a marble-floored area with a grand staircase and a chandelier as lovely as the one in our home. We were approaching the executive offices, I realized. At that moment, a handsome man, dressed like a gentleman's fashion magazine cover, introduced himself and offered us his hand. He led us into a grand conference room.

There we met with the company's four principal officers. These men had presence. You could literally feel the power that emanated from each one. This was nothing like our experiences in the other labs we had visited.

Fifteen minutes of our allotted time remained. My heart beat faster. How in the world could I share my vision in just fifteen minutes?

"My wife is a breast cancer survivor," Glenn began.

"Honey, can I talk for just a minute?" I interrupted, gently touching his arm. I meant to speak a little faster, to accomplish as much as we could in so short a time. But God helped me, and suddenly I saw all four of those men had tears in their eyes. They looked at me with such respect, and they were crying.

Two hours later we shook hands with the four gentlemen, who now were our friends. We had formed a deep bond. They had agreed to produce our products. Every one of us felt that special holy excitement that happens at rare times.

I must have talked ninety miles per hour as Glenn and I flew home to Dallas. I could hardly wait to get home, sit down at my desk and write a letter to those four gentlemen to thank them for their time. "Let's get started," I planned to say. "Let's do this, and that . . ." —and everything I had imagined during our flight.

But the Lord spoke to my heart. "I told you to be still and know that I am God. I told you to wait."

"But this is *it*, Lord. What in the world are You telling me?" I asked.

"You are not to do anything," God said.

That broke my heart. I literally felt heartbreak, but at last I said, "Yes, Lord." I said yes, but I surely did not understand Him. Two weeks later when I was praying one morning, God gave me the go-ahead. I then realized that God had tested my obedience. I had been so ready to call the next morning and say, "Go to work. Here's the check." Instead, God instructed me to do nothing.

When God did give the go-ahead, however, I immediately wrote a letter to the company's chairman. God really blessed that letter, and it was passed around among the other executives. That letter immediately took us beyond our initial business relationship and into something far more powerful and personal. These men became some of our best friends. The president's wife is my close friend and prayer partner. God obviously had given us favor with one another.

We were now on the fast track and the high-quality track for preparing our products for market. From time to time I flew out to the laboratory. Once I took Dr. Godat with me to advise us on the breast cream and hormone cream we were developing. Dr. Godat was enormously impressed by everything he saw at that high-level laboratory operation.

Another time when Glenn and I visited, we learned we must name our company and its product line. The lab's research department almost instantly can tell you if a suggested name is already in use. As we all worked together, it seemed that everything pertaining to nutrition was already taken. At last I came up with the name *Ultimate Living*, which we all loved.

We all applauded when the name passed the researcher's scrutiny. Hooray for our new company and product name! That was a milestone to celebrate.

So that's how *Ultimate Living International, Inc.* came to be named. I liked the way it echoes one of the most powerful truths Jesus uttered: "The thief comes only in order to steal and kill and destroy. I came that they may have and enjoy life, and have it in abundance (to the full, till it overflows)" (John 10:10).

The thief comes to bring cancer and other destructive assaults on our health. Ultimate Living, I decided, would help us all have health and life and have those gifts in abundance!

Another Test

Ultimate Living International, Inc. opened its doors in our Dallas headquarters on August 1, 1996. That day we officially introduced our Green Miracle, our flagship green food product that truly deserves the name Miracle. I'll tell about how that product came into its amazing existence in a later chapter.

As I write these lines, Ultimate Living has just celebrated our third anniversary. We primarily used Glenn's good credit rating to back our production and start-up costs. At the time of our opening, future products mostly were still in the planning or testing stage.

Today we have full lines of exceptionally high-quality nutritional and skin-care products. More than six thousand distributors in virtually every state in America, plus Hong Kong and Singapore, daily introduce more and more consumers to the benefits of these health-enhancing products. The news—and our territories—continue to spread.

It thrills me to see women establish their own home-based nutrition businesses. Women are guardians of a family's health. Get women sold on good nutrition, and the whole family begins to thrive. This is a fast-growing, amazingly successful young company. I am so very proud to be its spokesperson!

When we pray for my business, so often Glenn and I remember what my mother envisioned for me. "You will have a ministry," she said. "Your cancer experience will help guide you into helping other people everywhere." Glenn, who loved Mother dearly and credits her with being very instrumental in his Christian growth, calls her a true example of the woman God describes in Proverbs 31. My mother, I believe, would be the first to understand my experience—actually, my test—in Mexico, when the company was barely one year old.

In August 1997 I wanted to visit our lab, because I was working on some new nutritional supplements. Actually, that trip would serve two purposes. I would go to the laboratory, then into a hospital in Mexico where they were treating terminally ill cancer patients with some interesting alternative treatments. I had heard they were getting good results, but I wanted to see first hand.

Glenn and I were sitting with the hospital administrator. His office window looked out upon a little swimming pool, where I could see a patient, a little boy, sitting with his parents. The boy was young, perhaps five or six, and profoundly wasted by cancer. Hairless, weak, his tiny bones so prominent. "Tell me about that little boy," I asked the doctor.

He had been brought in suffering the final cancer stage, they told me.

"You have to tell me this little boy is going to live. Will he *live?* This little boy will die unless God heals him!" I exclaimed.

"You are right, Mrs. Simmons," the doctor said. "That little boy is going to die. He was brought to us too late, and I'm sure there's nothing you can do for him."

I asked to visit the other patients. We went from room to room. I remember a beautiful black girl of thirty and her mother. The mother was also beautiful. Her daughter had big tumors, and she was so weary. I put my arms around her and held her and started praying. I cannot tell you the burden God placed on my heart at that moment for that girl. And the other rooms were the same, with suffering people and my prayers.

As we crossed the Mexican border and returned to our hotel, the burden grew heavier and heavier on my heart. A heavy oppression like a dark cloud covered all of us. I was very quiet. Glenn and I were deposited at our hotel in the San Diego area. We were going to dinner that night with the vice president of our laboratory and his special lady. Usually that would be such a treat, but now all I wanted to do was get alone with God.

After dinner I could hardly wait to return to my room. It so happened we had a two-bedroom suite, so Glenn went to sleep in one room, and I tiptoed into the other. I lay on the floor and began to pray. Soon I began to weep and weep and weep.

I walked over to the big window that looked out on all that beauty and splendor, and I stared into the darkness as I prayed and cried, prayed and cried, all night long.

"God, I give it up," I sobbed. "I cannot do this. I cannot walk through this valley of the shadow of death. You know I have a company in Texas . . . that I talk to cancer patients on the telephone . . . and I'm doing what You told me to do. But I cannot go into areas like this. I can't do this, God. I cannot do this."

All night long I cried out to God and wrestled in my spirit. By 5:30 the next morning, exhausted as I was, I began to weep even more heavily. Then God spoke to me.

"My child, when I healed you and gave back your life to you, you made Me a promise. You cannot choose where you go, to whom you talk, to what parts of the world you travel or where you minister. I will lead and direct you.

142

"I will send you into the world, and it will not be easy. It will be hard. You must make your decision now. Will you give Me 100 percent as you once promised?"

The choice was mine. I knew I would go all the way with Him, or it would be nothing. By now it was six in the morning. I had prayed and wept all night long. As I surveyed the ocean through tired and scratchy eyes, I watched the waves rush in. The rising sun began to streak the waters with fingers of rose and gold. His creation looked glorious.

My soul was full. I knew it was now decision time. Was I willing to give my life and go into the whole world to serve others? Into territories I knew would not be pleasant, would be uncomfortable—even heart-breaking? In an instant, like a flash, I fell on my face and made that final commitment. My life must go from vision to victory. I would be a vehicle reaching out to others and, hopefully, help save lives.

Suddenly a heavenly language began to roll out of my mouth, rushing and rushing like the waves of the sea. And that awful burden, the dark depression, this heavy thing I had carried, was lifted off my shoulders. I prayed and worshiped, awed by the beauty of His presence and the glory of that fresh new morning. My heart was singing, "Yes, God, I will go to the end of the world with You. I will not question where You want me to go."

And He was telling me in my heart, "You must leave

your comfort zone. You will walk in the places where I walk. Today I have broken your heart with the things that break My heart. You will minister to people from all walks of life. You will serve the rich and the poor . . . everyone I call My own!"

I would walk through the valley of the shadow of death, I now understood, but I would fear no evil. God is with me. Those of us who face life and death for ourselves or those we love know there is a breaking time. There's a time to see what you really are made of . . . and if you are willing to pay the price of pushing through to where God wants you to be.

Through that night's experience God gave me an even greater passion for what I am called to do. He has given me a supernatural love for people. And He shows me again and again the greatness He has placed in others.

Filled with a new sense of peace, I sneaked into bed beside Glenn at six in the morning. At seven o'clock I shook him. "Honey, let's get up. Let's go have some breakfast," I told him. He never knew what had happened to me the night before. My heart felt too full to share these things with anyone, even Glenn.

Glenn had told me, "I know what God wants you to do." The nutrition company we envisioned then came into being, has spread out and prospered.

There is something God wants you to do. Finding that "something" becomes part of your ultimate living.

Eleven

Making Memories

MY FRIEND MARIAN BARNES brought me an exquisite present one day—a good-sized box, padded and covered in pure white brocade and trimmed with white silk cording.

"This is for your mother's love notes," she said.

Marian made that box for me. Only a friend as sensitive as Marian could have imagined, then created, such a precious gift. Now I can dip my hand into the box and pull out a message from my mother: "To my beautiful daughter, Diane. God knew I needed sunshine."

Or, "I love and thank you for everything you have done for me—especially as I thank the Lord for giving me you."

Those little notes instantly bring Mother's face, her laugh, her self back to me. The memories never are sad. They are loving and encouraging. Often they are funny. They are like balm to my soul.

Those instant mental snapshots—her broad, mischievous smile, the little pearl earrings, her ladylike ways and how she spent her life trying to make me into less of a tomboy—come back in a flash. Memories of my mother stay with me all the time. And of course, every time I open that box it also brings memories of Marian, who is very much alive and a big part of my life.

I remember when Marian and I went on a diet together. We decided we'd consume *nothing* that wouldn't go through a soda straw. Marian's husband, a prominent dentist, offered to wire our jaws shut, but we declined. (He was just kidding . . . I think!) Anyway, have you ever tried to suck tacos through a straw?

Let me share something with you. One of the best and most healing gifts we can give one another is that of making good memories. I believe God uses memories as a wonderful source of healing and comfort. He has given us the miraculous gift of memory so we can continually recall those people, places and times in our lives that make us happy and keep us focused.

Glenn makes fantastic memories for people. His four grandchildren don't know him as a powerful corporate director in a black suit and dark tie. They know the granddaddy who tramps around his ranch with them, teaches them to fish and shows them the little wild creatures on his property.

They remember the granddaddy who took them to Disney World and let them ride every ride and see every sight, took them to restaurants he'd never choose for himself and never once complained about being tired. Or hot. Or wishing he could take a nap.

Appreciation

It's about appreciating life, folks. Whether we are battling cancer or doing our own humdrum everyday thing, we need to decide to make good memories—a spiritual nest egg, if you will, for those we love.

Mother did that without thinking about it. All during our final four weeks and three days, she added to my storehouse of priceless memories. She instructed me: "Remember, Diane, to give the plan of salvation when you speak at my service." (I sure did, Mother, and we mailed out hundreds of tapes of the service in answer to requests. I spoke for forty-two minutes!)

She edified me: "God told me He would place my mantle onto you. You will minister around the world." (I had absolutely no picture of that.)

She reproved me: "No, Diane, I am not afraid to die. I'm going to heaven and will be with Jesus."

(Mother, I thought you could talk God out of that. I really wanted you to do that!)

Like many other cancer survivors, these days I doubly appreciate my life. I wanted to live. I love life. So do you, I'm sure. What I want us to do now, in appreciation of the life we have been given, is to deliberately decide on the memories we want others to inherit. If you want to take your daughter to New York City to see a ballet performance, do so. Go with her. Share her thrills. If you want your child to have peace with God through a personal relationship with Jesus Christ, do as my daddy did and help her pray the prayer of salvation. (What a memory that is!) In other words, make a real point of appreciating people and God's world and your own life. Do it now.

I'm not saying do these things or you will be sorry. I *am* saying, do the things that *last*—the father-son World Series tickets, the family cruise vacation, the big surprise party. Make good memories whenever you can. Good memories are real bargains. They outlast all the trials and tribulations of life and never fade, shrink or go out of style.

Let's show God and one another how much we appreciate our rich, abundant lives and the blessings He pours into them. The Jewish people have a wonderful toast: *L'Chaim!* That means, "To life!" Their collective memories contain many horrors, yet they still can appreciate God's goodness and mercy. Their wisdom has taught them to celebrate and commemorate, and this is a valuable lesson for people of all faiths.

To appreciate means to gain in value or worth. Let's appreciate life. Let's pack it full of wonderful memories.

Healing Hidden Emotions

It was the fifth anniversary of my mother's home going. I was on my way to visit some precious older people in a nursing home and discovered I was early. Suddenly I turned my car around and took the road that led to Mother's gravesite.

This was not planned. In fact, I had not been to Restland since her death. This bothered Glenn a lot. He sensed I had not really faced the grieving process and felt that my avoiding the cemetery signaled that I still had some real grief work to do. Daddy visited her grave, of course, and Glenn did, too. But I wouldn't go. She was not there, I told them. She is in heaven.

My mother had been buried in a new part of Restland, a section just opened up. Now this section was filled in as far as the eye could see. I felt like a lost child. I didn't know where to go. I parked my car, got out and began to walk, becoming so frustrated, confused and upset because there was nothing with which I could identify. I stopped and thought, *I must find my car. This is like a bad dream. I must leave.*

It was as if a voice said, "No. Be still."

I stopped and said, "OK, God. If You want me to find my mother's grave You'll have to show me where it is. I am a lost child."

Then I just went . . . with no map or direction. I looked down, and there was her grave. Meanwhile, the bright, sunny sky began to get dark, dark, dark, and a heaviness and oppression came over me. I looked up, and black clouds were swirling and swirling above me, yet there was no rain.

I began to talk to my mother aloud. "Mother! How could you have left me? I don't know what to do. I don't have anyone like you in whom to confide. I miss your spiritual wisdom. Glenn is a godly man and a wonderful Christian, but I don't have you.

"You always told me what to do, Mother. You've always been there for me. I'd always ask you what to do, and God gave you such divine wisdom. Now you're not here, and I miss you so much!

"You can't imagine these past five years . . . working eighteen hours a day. I'm doing what you told me to do. You said I had to carry on your work of helping people. I had to make a difference in people's lives. I've done all that, Mother, plus more, but I miss you so much, and there will never be anyone else who can fill that void. What am I going to do?"

I talked to my mother for thirty minutes. Suddenly, it seemed our conversation was over. I told her how much I loved her. I told her how much I missed her. My face turned up to heaven, I prayed to God . . . speaking to Him, but to my mother, too.

At that, I looked up at the sky again, and the dark clouds were gone. It was brilliantly sunny now. My spirit had lifted. The oppression was gone. Every burden had been lifted off my shoulders, and I felt *free*—an indescribably free and joyous feeling.

During that short hour God brought the heavy suitcase full of grief and unexpressed emotions I had been carrying to a place of full closure. Complete closure. I had pushed those deep, hidden feelings down for five years, but that day, beside my mother's grave, they finally surfaced. God almost instantly healed all my confusion and pain! I then fully accepted the responsibilities Mother had placed on my shoulders.

What has this to do with making memories?

Hidden emotions can block and stifle the very memories we most yearn to retrieve. When we can free those emotions, we also can free many tender recollections that we will cherish forever.

Ask God to help you deal with any hidden emotions that still feel too painful to confront. His gentle surgery will heal your heart, your spirit and your life.

Making Memories Breast Cancer Foundation

On July 10, 1999, a limousine arrived at the Brasstown Bald Mountain Resort in Young Harris, Georgia, and Nancy Kelly emerged. This was the perfect place for Nancy's family reunion, you would agree. The gorgeous new resort hotel sits high atop Brasstown Bald, a famous Georgia landmark. It commands a breathtaking view of the rolling Blue Ridge Mountain range. The air felt cool. Breezes carried the scent of lush cedars and pines. A great bald eagle swooped low, signaling to its mate.

We knew this reunion of Nancy's family members from Nevada, Florida, Tennessee, Alabama, North Carolina, South Carolina and Georgia would be a once-in-a-lifetime occasion.

Nancy Kelley has metastatic cancer. The fifty-year-old wife, mother, school principal and local newspaper columnist fought a good fight, but her cancer advanced even faster. Nancy's greatest wish was to see her family reunited for a wonderful weekend retreat—all thirty-one men, women and children!

That's where the Making Memories Breast Cancer Foundation came in. This new nonprofit organization is dedicated to granting the important wishes of women in final-stage breast cancer. Results are phenomenal. I get to see with my own eyes the amazing effects happiness creates in the patient.

I was excited to be there in spirit as national spokesperson for the Making Memories Breast Cancer Foundation.

From limousine to wheelchair, Nancy was escorted with real fanfare. Someone placed a bouquet of flowers in her arms. A song written in her honor was sung. The Young Harris mayor proclaimed it Nancy Kelly Day, and the proclamation was read aloud. The press arrived. A professional cameraman videotaped the occasion. And for three days, Nancy's family laughed, cried, joked and reminisced, just like any other large family on vacation. They must have taken a million snapshots.

Watching this family interact, people were struck by the power of "memory making." So much was going on within this close-knit group. Within an hour following her arrival, Nancy Kelly had ditched her wheelchair and was visiting, pulling her oxygen tank behind her.

The idea is to tap into the happiness factor. Create some meaningful memories. Draw families closer together. Forget worries and sadness for a while. And Nancy's reunion succeeded beyond our wildest dreams.

Nancy was realistic about her condition. Her greatest need and desire, obviously, was to achieve closure. She accomplished this through creating a happy, heartwarming, emotionally satisfying occasion that allowed thirty-one family members to enjoy her and one another.

This is what our foundation aims to do. Most younger families run out of money long before costly cancer treatment expenses can be met. There are absolutely no funds available for them to spend on "happy endings." And women with metastatic breast cancer desperately want to leave a legacy. One woman wants to plant a shade tree, a memorial that will shelter her growing family. Another asks for a video camera so she can be taped while speaking individual love messages to her family members.

Then there's the young mother of five-year-old

153

twin boys, and the other who has three children under age twelve. Both of these women desire family trips to Disney World.

Sick as they are, these women make heroic efforts to minister to their families. Intuitively, they know the importance of making wonderful memories. Every instinct in them is proclaiming *L'Chaim!* To life!

In early 1999 a mutual friend introduced me to Fran Hansen, the Portland, Oregon, woman who conceived and founded this great program and serves as its executive director. Fran got the idea in December 1997 when doctors told her she might have breast cancer. While waiting for the diagnosis, she scoured the Internet to find out more about the disease. In chat rooms, she read first-person accounts from terminally ill women.

"Some of these letters really gripped my heart," she said. "After I was found OK, I imagined those women who were told, 'You do have breast cancer.'"

I immediately caught Fran's vision. That powerful wish-granting weekend in Georgia reinforced it for me. Until cures for breast cancer can be found, we women must stand together. We are suffering far too many battle casualties. We must close ranks and make a positive stand. Making Memories Breast Cancer Foundation intends to remind us that these are women. Not statistics.

I feel so proud to serve as their spokesperson. Fran Hansen explains, "The tragedy of metastatic breast cancer, as with any terminal disease, is not only the physical and emotional impact, but the toll on the family." Her vision is simple: "To make a difference in the families affected by helping them to put reality aside, if only for a few days, and allowing loved ones to spend quality time together."

This is a grass roots volunteer effort, still in its infancy. We have no foundation grants or funds other than those donated by people like you and me. But individuals are responding by donating a time-share week, frequent-flyer miles and other travel funds. So many women long for a second honeymoon. Others want airline tickets to bring a son or daughter home.

Those of us who have survived breast cancer and those who have lost friends or loved ones to this disease will want to support the cause. What a fitting and practical living memorial!

Nancy Kelly agrees. "Except for experiencing peace with God through faith in Jesus Christ, my marriage and the birth of our son, this was the next most exciting event of my lifetime," she wrote.

Let's begin to make more good memories for ourselves and those we love. And above all, let's help our brave terminal cancer patients make marvelous memories now.

The Mickie Gee Fireside Room and Garden

"Have I told you lately that I love you? I really do, every hour of every day. Mother."

155

Mother and Daddy loved not just me and my siblings, but thousands of others they met through their church. At age eighty-two, my daddy is still one of the most respected leaders in that church. He and Mother invested much of their lives in serving there.

As time passed following Mother's death, Glenn asked me, "Don't you think we should find some way to honor your mother?" It didn't take much thinking to decide we should donate a memorial of some kind to her church.

That large, growing church was about to add a sizeable new wing to the sanctuary. We thought of donating a library, since Mother so enjoyed reading. As we prayed and considered it even more, the idea of a lovely meeting room that opened onto a formal garden began to take shape.

We wanted something very versatile and functional, yet elegant and inviting. This would be a place appropriate for a small wedding, reception, missionary meeting or dozens of other uses. It would be a special space, one as lovely as my mother herself, I dreamed. People would feel welcome and happy there, and the garden beyond would be equally lovely and enjoyable.

The decorator the church chose came to my house to get a feel for the colors and objects I liked. I wanted Mother's room to be almost an extension of the calm, formal feeling our home projects. Soon we were deep into colors, fabrics and furniture selections. I began to get excited!

Everything came together as smoothly as if God were guiding the project—and He was. A large fireplace became the room's focal point. A grand portrait of my parents hangs above the fireplace, and there's a beautiful plaque that describes my mother's life.

The room lends itself to many different seating arrangements. An adjoining kitchen makes it possible to hold dinners. They can have musical programs there, as well, or almost any other kind of function. It became such a beautiful, beautiful room. It looks like my mother.

Then you can step out beneath the canopy and enter the small, enclosed garden. There's a little fountain where the birds can play (Mother loved birds) and benches where people can take a quiet rest. Gorgeous shrubbery and colorful flowers grace this garden all year. There's such a feeling of peace in Mother's fireside room and her perfect little garden, and I know she would love everything about it. Most of all, she would love the idea of sharing those lovely surroundings with the people God sends there. I know those people can feel Mother's love.

Another thing she would like is that the decorator who helped create the room eventually received a breast cancer diagnosis—and I was able to help walk her through her decision-making about her treatment options. My mother would like that even more than the room itself!

In August 1998 we held a dinner in the *Mickie Gee*

Fireside Room and Garden and dedicated those spaces to the Lord. Glenn, Daddy and I could certainly feel Mother's presence with us. It was a very happy occasion in a very happy room, and my mother, who specialized in making people happy, would have loved every minute of it.

To God be the glory for all the good memories that room will hold!

Twelve

Prosperity and Good Health

I BELIEVE THAT IN REALITY ONLY one disease exists—that of a broken-down immune system. Scientists have long believed that after age twenty the human immune system begins to wane, slowly dwindling each year after that until death. The good news is, we now know it doesn't have to be that way. In recent years medical science has determined that we can enhance, and in some cases even rebuild, faulty immune defenses.

159

The human immune system ranks as the most sophisticated protective apparatus ever designed. Billion-dollar warning, defense and guidance systems developed for NASA and NATO don't hold a candle to what has been built into you. Your immune system will determine how long you will live and how well you will live while you are alive.

This wonderful defense system protects every tissue, membrane, muscle, gland, blood vessel, bone . . . even each individual cell. It is designed to protect us from disease from without (bacterial and viral infections) and attacks from within (tumors and cancers, for example).

It's exciting to learn ways we can build up, strengthen and preserve those important defenses no matter what age we happen to be, or in what stage of illness or health. The fact is, it is never too late to help ourselves prosper.

We're learning a lot these days about how to boost human immunity. We know what threatens it: stress, continuing anxiety states, anger, free radicals, certain food additives, poisonous environmental conditions, smoking, drugs, alcohol abuse and other common factors. We also know a great deal about how to head off damage from such elements, and how to restore our immune system to health once such damage has occurred.

But there's more. We also possess something designed to protect that vulnerable immune system.

And what is this built-in guardian for our most basic and often-threatened protection system, our immunity? It's the life-giving, overcoming, built-in power of the human spirit!

You read a lot these days about the mind-body connection in relation to health and healing. Studies have demonstrated how powerfully the mind can influence the body—for better or for worse. Some people dismiss such ideas as nonsense. Other thoughtful researchers point out that the brain directs every bodily movement and function and every subtle emotion in our physical makeup. The brain tells our hearts how to beat. It regulates our internal temperature. It teaches our flesh to heal, tells us when to eat and sleep and signals us to laugh or produce tears.

The brain, therefore, plays a vital and complex role in directing the immune responses that determine how well we live, fend off diseases and heal from physical assaults.

The first authority figure to teach that there can be no perfect health unless we aim toward wholeness was God. Obviously we cannot be almost healthy or almost prosperous. God wants us whole—or holy. The Scriptures were instructing us in these concepts long before modern alternative medicine's ideas, including that of holistic medicine, came along. Those concepts worked then, and they work now.

Let's see how building a strong immune system, and learning to use that powerful mind-body connection, fits

161

into our pictures. And what about the word *prosperity?*

Prosperity

To prosper, in the sense we're using the word, means to use a health method or dietary supplement that makes you bloom and thrive. It's an old farmer's term: "I tried this new fertilizer, and my corn crop prospered."

I was searching for that exact form of health-giving prosperity when I formulated my first product, *Green Miracle.* Remember that bottle of green powder I discovered in my kitchen drawer soon after my cancer surgery? Well, I had begun taking that supplement, which is based on highly nutritious barley and other greens, right away.

In the years that followed, as I read and studied nutrition and interviewed some of the world's foremost nutritional experts, I began adding other essential elements to my basic diet. My kitchen counters overflowed with all the bottles and jars! The total cost per month was staggering.

By now I knew many companies were making such green food supplements. This is one of the most important cornerstones of all nutrition, in my opinion, so I gave a lot of thought as to how these valuable green products could be improved. How could I standardize the milligram count received in a single portion? Also, some of these products featured one green plant food, such as barley, while others offered two or three.

How much vital, basic nutrition could be crammed into one product? How could we standardize these ingredients so the consumer knew exactly what he or she received each time? And would it be possible to combine a day's basic nutritional elements into one powerful product?

The more I studied these questions, the more excited I became. By the time I took these challenges to our laboratories, in fact, I thought I had it all figured out. I expected to receive the results of all my work in about a month.

"God, I want a green food that can produce miracles!" I had prayed. So I took all the vital ingredients, all the green foods, and the vision God gave me to create a product for the world.

After much prayer, study and work—it took our laboratory several months to make this sophisticated product to my specifications—we created what I believe to be the world's most complex and effective blend of plant foods, fibers and other nutritional elements. It truly is a miracle.

Green Miracle, as we named it, contains more than fifty ingredients. Few people could afford to purchase them singly. Nutritionists urge us to eat five fruits and vegetables per day. This supplement contains, in one day's portion, the nutritional equivalent of the fruits and vegetables needed for the day. It is nutrition packed! If there is a better product of this sort anywhere, I will change this formula tomorrow.

Green Miracle was designed to promote not just adequate good health, but an abundance of vigor, stamina and immune system buildup. We want you not just to improve your health, but to overflow with physical prosperity—the ultimate living we believe God desires for each of us.

I take Green Miracle, of course. Not only did I develop it, but I believed in it long before I held the finished product in my hands. I would skip brushing my teeth in the morning before I would leave off my Green Miracle!

This is not meant to be a testimonial. (Remember, I do not prescribe.) But I want to illustrate two vitally important points: First, it might take hard work and real determination to find and adopt the best health-enhancing lifestyle possible, and second, you will be thrilled with the results!

Unfortunately, too few women approaching sixty, seventy and eighty have anything like the energy, vigor, bright eyes and glowing skin we can and should have. Remember, even if you are sick today, you can have those benefits tomorrow! It's your decision.

Also, too many women in their fifties, forties and even younger are stressed to the breaking point—and it shows. You know you should be at the height of your beauty, strength and radiance right now—and you know you're not. Take courage, friend.

In my late forties I discovered I had cancer. Today, nearing the big 6-0, I look and feel and act a bunch younger than I did twelve years ago.

We can reverse that mediocre health picture. We can head off cancers and other death-dealing enemies. We can restore our bodies to radiant health after conquering the worst physical challenges. I know of breast cancer survivors who not only regain their great health, but go on to become actresses and fashion models. We don't have to lose our looks.

So shed the pounds, strengthen the immune system and add on the new energy and beauty. There's no way to describe the self-respect you'll gain or the new respect your husband, son and daughter show you. You're setting them and others an excellent example. It warms my heart to know that D'Andra thinks I look great (You're pretty gorgeous yourself, sweetie!) and thanks me for setting a good example.

That's so important. All mothers want our children to prosper and be in good health. And every wife wants her husband looking, thinking and feeling fabulous. Glenn, who watched my stock of vitamins and other supplements accumulating on the kitchen counter over the years, never would read any of the fascinating nutritional books and papers I so enjoyed.

However, when I laid out the supplements for him each day, he faithfully took them. Each quarter when he gets his blood work done he gets a good report. Not bad for a hard-working youngster of seventy-one! He's holding on to his good looks, too, I keep telling him.

Our nation for some time has enjoyed a period of

great financial prosperity. How strange, then, that so few of us—women, especially—can honestly call ourselves physically and emotionally prosperous. More than half of our population is seriously overweight. Meanwhile, stress-induced diseases like coronary artery disease and various cancers continue to strike more and more of us.

Let's get off the slow track. Let's get off the candidate-for-illness list, too. Instead, let's become the female Pied Piper who leads her friends and her entire family toward better health and more prosperity. When you do, I want to hear your story. I am interested.

In the past, few ventured to believe anything about healing beyond what their doctors told them. Today, ask a doctor about biblical healing principles, and most physicians will agree that they work. Many believe an individual's faith encourages a better, quicker healing, that prayer becomes a valuable asset and that the laying on of hands calms and relaxes a patient prior to surgery.

Physicians and surgeons often relate instances of patients receiving miracle healings—phenomena for which the medical community can offer no plausible explanation.

It was not hard for me to accept that concept, which goes beyond traditional medicine with all its benefits. Alternative healing approaches used as adjuncts to standard medical practices simply combine "the best of nature with the best of science."

Alternative medicine largely centers around a sophisticated knowledge and use of nutrition. Historically the American medical community has mostly ignored nutrition as a realistic aid to healing and relied instead on its enormous repertoire of prescription drugs. Too often the use of these medicines, including many common over-the-counter remedies, results in side effects that damage our immune defenses.

More than any other people on earth, Americans depend upon doctor-prescribed remedies. Because chemotherapy and radiation therapy for cancers, strong painkillers for arthritis and countless other well-known prescription drugs are so powerful, it is essential that we take careful charge over our immune system and do all we can to strengthen it.

Certainly drugs save lives. In doing so, however, they too often wreak havoc on our bodies. Before entering into chemotherapy, radiation therapy or any other long-term protocol that requires medicine's biggest guns, it pays to consult nutritionists with the best credentials you can find.

Show your nutritionist all your prescription drugs. Ask for a recommended reading list, and begin to learn, learn and learn. This is the start of your lifelong learning plan. Someday your new knowledge could save a life. Undoubtedly it should increase not only your quality of life, but perhaps its number of years as well.

Before adding any supplements to your diet—vitamins, minerals, fiber, herbs—be sure your primary physician knows about them. Sometimes these can conflict with prescribed medications or heighten or diminish your prescriptions' effects.

Dr. Peters always OK'd my supplements. He did not always agree with what I was doing, but he did monitor everything I took to make sure I did myself no harm.

Physicians often specialize. Perhaps it's too much to expect them to become highly knowledgeable about nutrition in addition to the specialty it took them years to learn. But more and more often, doctors are taking a broader approach. Nowadays you may even find a physician who is willing to try a natural remedy first, before resorting to prescription drugs.

If so, cherish your doctor. You can work together, learn together and probably may help other patients in the process. Our health knowledge base has increased enormously during the past decade. The future looks even brighter.

Good Health

It takes years, sometimes decades, for a cancer to become visible. The day Dr. Godat discovered that lump in my breast, we both knew this was no new cancer. It had silently established itself, cell by multiplying cell, over a period of years before we could see it.

The good news is, even years of bad and careless health habits need not permanently affect your body's good functioning. Look around and you'll see plenty of others who, like me, not only have fully regained their health, but actually are healthier than before. Our bodies actually are capable of fighting off some formidable diseases. I have known many people who, when given three or six months to live, defied the doctor's prognosis and, after the fight of their lives, returned to excellent health.

As we have learned, high-quality nutrition and the best dietary supplements go a long way in promoting healing and life-long well-being. But there's also another kind of divine nourishment science knows to be amazingly effective: good human relationships.

It seems that the healthiest human beings are those who have many authentic friendships and relation-ships. Contacts with others actually boost the immune system, while loneliness and isolation are known to lower our defenses.

Various studies have proven that our physical health and emotional health are intertwined. The more links we add to our chain of family, friends and others, the healthier we seem to become. And as we grow older, cancer risks become greater. Could that relate in part to a decrease in our circle of human contacts?

Charlie Brown, the Peanuts comic strip character, says, "I need all the friends I can get." Medical science agrees with him. One of the best-known ways to strengthen the immune system is to strengthen our social life. It is important, even when we are battling a

169

chronic illness, that we make a real effort to maintain our ties to others and not become a social dropout.

We need touching, too. We never outgrow that need. We know that babies who are starved for human touch fail to thrive. In fact, psychologists claim all of us need fifteen touches a day for good emotional health. These days most of us move way too fast to stop for that many hugs, pats or kisses. But what would happen to our stress levels if we did stop? Would our health improve?

When Marian rubbed my feet, I know she helped me heal. And when I pray with a stranger who is terrified about his or her cancer diagnosis, I feel God's message go from my lips to that person's ears. I can feel God filling that person's heart with fresh hope.

Visits and prayers with my family and friends were the greatest blessings I experienced during my recovery. Those lights of love made my days so much brighter. No words could ever do justice to the joy and love I feel in my heart for those precious ones. They were my comfort and my emotional support. When I look at those loved ones I see a reflection of God's love.

Does love actually have the power to nourish and heal? Absolutely! Even Christina, my tiny poodle dog, loved me unceasingly while I was healing. With every beat of her little heart I could feel waves of unconditional love, pure love and wonderful doggie devotion. Emotional nourishment from dogs and cats is such a real asset to sick or lonely people that pets, including Christina, are often taken into nursing homes to spread love and fun among seniors.

During my own cancer crisis and recovery I know God used many people who brought harmony and love into my life. This taught me the importance of speaking and writing words of encouragement and love to others when they go through times of crisis and challenge.

Never try to go it alone. You need the love of others fully as much as you need the medicines your doctor prescribes, and maybe even more. Sickness can make us feel broken down and defenseless, but other people's love and encouragement can rebuild our inner person at times when we believe that's impossible.

Reach out to that love and accept it.

Deeper Relationship

One of the good things a cancer experience accomplishes is to deepen our awareness of others. In my own family, many things changed after I had cancer. Our family's relationships became a priority as never before.

When Mother died from cancer, we declared all-out war against the disease. We would fight for others who had it. Even at times when we felt as though we were sinking under our grief, our family actually was pulling together and becoming closer than ever. We had always been loving and demonstrative, but now we became more so. We became more patient with

171

one another, less hurried and began speaking words of love even more often.

This is the healthiest, most prosperous way to live. What a blessing to enjoy the kind of family where everyone learns to thrive . . . to experience ultimate living.

God wants us to live that way. Some of us must change the ways we relate, the ways we think and speak and learn to become more open to receiving the love and encouragement so basic to our health. Many cancer patients learn to do just that. They learn how to thrive. After their healing, they know they are much stronger human beings.

I know. I am one of those people.

The Ultimate Connection

I see a cancer diagnosis as a wake-up call that thrusts us into battle against a death-dealing invader. Our fortress—our body—has come under attack and been invaded. Our first job is to learn how to nourish and supply ammunition to the body so it can fight off the invaders and become immune to future attacks.

Then we must seek an even stronger source of nourishment from the army of friends, relatives and other associates who go with us into battle. They become our powerful reinforcements whenever we feel as though we may faint or fall.

But the ultimate line of defense, in my experience, is that of joining my spirit with that of the living God.

172

He has made me, and He knows how to make me once again into a brand-new creature.

It is not God's will for you or me to be sick. It is His will for us to be well, healthy, whole and strong. If you don't believe this, you need to change your thinking. God has not made you sick.

Cancer often makes people angry or bitter toward God. When these feelings surface, we should immediately pray: "God, I have been wrong. I have been blaming You, and I am sorry. You never send sickness to Your children. I have blamed You, and I now release this bitterness to You. Please forgive me."

It is essential that we free our heart from anger and bitterness toward God or anyone else, so that our prayers may not be hindered, but will prevail. If we ever have needed a clear channel toward our loving heavenly Father, we need it now. Anger and bitterness must not interfere.

A letter from a Texas physician gives a good prescription for achieving physical prosperity and spiritual and physical good health. "It took me three years to fight back from a near-fatal attack of cancer," he wrote. "Throughout the victorious struggle, I have tried to keep three elements of my healing triangle in balance. These would be:

1. The best available from modern medicine;
2. a proactive nutrition program, implemented with the help of a qualified nutritionist; and

173

3. an intensive program of mind/body spirituality that embraces a regimen of prayer, meditation and guided imagery.

"I tell new patients that inquire after my successful effort that cancer is a good news-bad news situation. The good news is that there is no law of the physical sciences that requires one to die of cancer. The bad news is that beating it is going to require a focused effort and more discipline than the average person has ever imagined." Fortunately, the latter is within the capability of anyone who has the determination to live.

"It is totally within the patient's own control, and nobody will ever send a bill for it."

Thirteen

Dee Simmons'
Health Regimen

"I TAKE GOOD CARE OF MYSELF."

That's my answer when people ask, "What do you do to get all that energy? Or, look as good as you do? How do you stay so young?"

People often ask those questions. Frankly, I love it. It's normal for a woman to have a little vanity, and everyone likes to hear kind comments.

But in another way, it disturbs me. Twelve years ago my breast cancer experience taught me that life is not a rehearsal. This is it, right now! I can choose to live it to the fullest or sit on the sidelines and watch it go by.

I chose life and living—*ultimate living.* I made a serious vow to God, Glenn and me. I would take charge over my life, my health and myself. What disturbs me is that it took cancer to make me do it. What further disturbs me is that other women often comment on the results, as though what I am achieving is so rare and unusual that it's beyond most people's capabilities.

Optimum health and ultimate living should not be all that rare and unusual in our wealthy nation. But look around and count how many fantastic examples you see in any crowded room. Far, far too few.

I'm not holding myself up as a perfect example, by the way. This is the reformed doughnut-and-pie junkie, remember? But I do go around constantly reminding myself and others that tomorrow's health is built on what we do today.

Today's smallest decisions can make a major impact on how well we think, feel, act, perform and look ten years from today. That's an obvious fact, of course, but one few people ever seem to consider. But ten years from today—possibly much sooner—you and I could be one of those super-healthy and vibrant individuals who seem to have it all. I'm getting there!

Question: How many women do you know who are bursting with good health, energy and well-being? Women who seem ageless? Women who operate from a state of excellence?

Next Question: So what's stopping the rest of us?

Whenever I fall off the wagon and find myself driving into the nearest Krispy Kreme parking lot, those questions resurface. In fact, I ponder them often. You see, I tell myself as I bite into that warm, golden circle of sugar-crusted goodness, the only difference between me and the reigning Miss Universe is spelled D-I-S-C-I-P-L-I-N-E. Miss Universe is not sitting in a hot parking lot trying to keep bits of icing off her suit and her car seat.

All kidding aside, that's why I developed a weekly health regimen for myself that never varies (not usually, anyway). This is a written schedule that has evolved over the years since my cancer experience. It has become so familiar I could almost follow it while sleepwalking. It is so much a part of my life that I couldn't do without it. It creates the structure, heightened awareness and measurable results I so desperately needed before cancer.

Today I am healthy and energetic. My cancer is gone. My health and fitness levels continue to climb. I intend to keep it that way.

But this is not about me. Let's talk about you. And let's get to work on the plan you need in order to reach your physical, mental and spiritual peak. We'll use my routine as a rough guide for yours . . . and perhaps we can coach one another and improve it even more.

Some people just live. I want to help you live well. Let's get started.

Making a Plan

Without a road map, we won't reach our destination. It's incredible how many of us just jump into our lives and truck on down the freeway. We too often race our motors and too seldom stop for any reason except to refuel. I had plenty of time to think about these things while I recuperated from cancer surgery. That's when I began planning my new regimen and putting it into action. Where you are is where you begin.

First, a little motivation. Every woman knows when she looks great. Knowing we look our best makes us stand a little taller and put some extra pizzazz into our walk, talk and facial expressions. We feel good. We laugh. We sparkle.

Hold the picture, because that's where we're heading. If you are a bank executive/soccer mom/home-maker/community leader who is suffering from burnout and exhaustion and know your health is being compromised, maybe you can't imagine it. If you are a grandmother with breast cancer, high blood pressure and depression it might seem all but hopeless. But trust me, it is not.

I have seen many lives going the wrong way on a one-way Health Street turn around and head toward Miracle Street. My own regimen began with my fears. I *feared* another bout of cancer. I *feared* and believed my immune system must be inadequate. I *feared* sickness and death. But those fears motivated me to develop a maximum anticancer defense system for myself.

This includes not only my new health maintenance habits, but new spiritual and emotional disciplines as well. For example, when I see a lump, bump or bruise on my body and fear rises up in me, I have learned to face it with fact and with faith. The good result is, I take myself to the doctor immediately, learn the facts and ease my mind. Beyond that, I *choose* to face each episode with faith, not terror. Since I still have fibrocystic disease in my breasts, these episodes occur periodically. I have had to change my attitude toward cancer from one of fear to that of overwhelming confidence in God, my doctors and myself.

What I urge all of us to do is to build up our defenses in every way. I want you to get your hopes up and keep them up. Then I want each of us to make a no-nonsense commitment to making our lives and health profiles abundant and exceptional.

Here's how I do it.

Dee's Regimen

5:30 A.M.   Rise and shine. Drink one 8-oz. glass of pure water.

5:45 A.M.   2 oz. of Ultimate Living's Ezzeac Plus tea.

179

6–6:30 A.M. I walk for two miles around the neighborhood, enjoying the weather, fresh air and flowers.

6:45 A.M. This is our daily Bible reading and prayer time for Glenn and me—even if one of us is out of town. We start our day together.

7:30 A.M. Time for my morning drink, which includes:

3 scoops Ultimate Living's Green Miracle
1 tsp. Vitamin C (2,000 mg.)
1 Tbsp. Omega oils
2 Tbsp. fresh-ground flaxseed
$\frac{1}{2}$ tsp. Ultimate Living's Ionic Trace Minerals
$\frac{1}{2}$ ripe banana
1 c. organic apple juice
a few organic blueberries
a small amount of pure water

I put these into a blender and whirl into a delicious drink.

I also take these vitamins:

2 Ultimate Living's Super Antioxidants
2 Ultimate Living's multivitamin capsules
3 Ultimate Living Cal-Mag Plus
1 Coenzyme Q_{10} (100 mg.)

Ultimate Living's Green Miracle is so packed with nutrients, plant foods, chlorophyll, vitamins, antioxidant factors, dietary fiber, vegetables rich in phytonutrients, herbal extracts and enzymes for digestion that there's nothing quite like it. Green Miracle contains numerous whole foods.

This green food actually represents a new generation of optimum nutrition. It curbs the appetite and improves elimination. Green Miracle contains no dairy, yeast or animal ingredients. It is suitable for vegetarians. I called it life's blood transfusion, or a health-food store in a can.

8:45 A.M.   I drink a 12-oz. glass of organic vegetable juice, with eight vegetables, freshly juiced.

All that potent nutrition, exercise and spiritual nourishment sure starts the day off right! Take time for doing things for God, your family and yourself, and you can handle whatever the day may hold. Incidentally, my morning's nutrition intake more than supplies my immune system's maximum needs . . . but I don't stop there.

9 A.M.   I arrive at my office, well-prepared for the day ahead. My secretary places a 12-oz. glass of pure water on my desk every hour. Remember, the regimen I'm describing has enabled me to

maintain the energy and stamina it takes to manage, develop and grow a company with more than six thousand associates . . . juggle a heavy travel schedule . . . make regular radio and television appearances . . . fill platform speaking dates . . . minister to and encourage hundreds, even thousands, of cancer patients one on one.

Some days are unbelievably hectic, but all that nutrition keeps me from sagging. For a midmorning snack I might eat a piece of fruit.

1 P.M. Lunch always features a salad and steamed veggies. If you do a lot of restaurant dining, these are always available. As for salad dressings and butter, let your conscience be your guide. Good, fresh food, cooked to perfection, does not need extras like butter and heavy sauces in my opinion. After lunch I have two more Ultimate Living's multiple vitamins and two more Ultimate Living's Super-Antioxidants.

3 P.M.   I drink 4 oz. of pure water with three scoops of Green Miracle, and I also enjoy a snack of sunflower seeds, almonds or organic dried apricots.

6:30 P.M.   For dinner, I choose grilled fish or a small portion of organic meat with lots of fresh vegetables and a crisp salad on the side. Very often pasta is on the menu, too.

9:30 P.M.   I sip a cup of herbal tea.

10 P.M.   Bedtime. Just before retiring, I take three Ultimate Living's Cal-Mag Plus.

Every day I drink at least one and one-half gallons of pure water. You need half your body weight in water each day. (Divide your body weight in pounds by two to get the number of ounces of water required.) Four times each year I use Ultimate Living's Fiber Cleanse to clean the colon. I also occasionally take colonics and chelation treatments, and I have one or two massages per week.

When I tell seminar attendees about my routine, questions and arguments fly thick and fast. "I don't have time." "I can't discipline myself." "Who can realistically spend that much time, money and effort on herself?" Let's take these objections in order.

Not having sufficient time for daily exercise,

183

scheduled prayer and Bible reading and fortifying oneself with the right food and nutritional supplements is nonsense. Women are the family's appointed caregivers. But if we don't first care for ourselves—in fact, make self care a priority—how can we adequately care for our family?

Many women seem unable to grasp that concept. They pour themselves out in service to everyone else but themselves, which at first seems noble and unselfish. At some point, however, life will ask them a pointed question: How long can you continue to pour from an empty bucket?

It is prudent, right and very wise to take all the time you need to strengthen your body, mind and spirit. The investment in yourself will spill over and benefit every other person you love. And only when you love yourself fully can you fully love others.

"I can't discipline myself" usually means that we, with all good intentions, put everyone else's concerns ahead of our own. That means that in all the flurry of family activities we don't manage to make time to work out our own best strategies. I first began thinking about my own disciplines at a time when all I had to do was lie in bed while healing from surgery, watching video movies with Marian and sipping tea—the only idle period in my adult life.

Schedule time to plan your regimen. Take the next step, and write it down on paper. Notice that I set a definite time for each step of my personal plan. Once you commit your decisions to writing and set a time line for each activity, the rest is easy.

Your plan won't fail—unless you fail to plan. Take the steps outlined above, however, and I guarantee you will have no problem with self-discipline. You will be able to live up to the important promises you made to yourself.

The question of how we can "realistically" spend so much time, money and effort on ourselves refers directly to our level of self-worth. Do we believe we actually are worth that much time, money and effort? It's always revealing to consider that question, and the real answer may shock you: It is realistic to believe you deserve to be healthy; it is OK to bless yourself.

God created us, according to the Bible, only a little lower than the angels. He has paid the ultimate price for you and me and every other individual in the world. We need to value ourselves more and raise our mental price tags.

Do the math. Which costs more—the money and time you'll spend on superb nutrition, exercise, prayer and study, or the extravagant costs in time, pain and cash a deadly disease can require? The correct answer is: Maximizing your health by practicing preventive medicine is the best bargain around!

Remember, your current level of health is a perfect reflection of your genetics reacting to the way you live and take care of yourself. If you are not satisfied with the health you have created, no problem. Simply

185

change the way you live—your lifestyle—and you will see an immediate change in your total health picture.

Your body can heal itself completely. It has the ability, but it needs your assistance. It is your responsibility—and mine—to learn how to help ourselves heal. I have studied that question for a dozen years. During that time I have survived cancer, researched the human immune system and learned ways to enhance it. Next I founded a cutting-edge nutritional supplement company that produces a full range of clinically pure products packed with essential natural elements proven to boost the immune system and maximize our general health.

A strong interest in the role nutrition plays in the fight against cancer might have remained purely theoretical, however, except that God kept sending me human health problems that needed solutions.

These human health questions arrived in the form of women named Betty, Joyce, Beth, Kay, Colleen, Rebecca and many, many others. He has allowed me to meet and involve myself with thousands who need my specialized knowledge and ministry. They are not "cancer problems" that need solving, but women whose names and faces come to my memory whenever I pray.

My role has been, first of all, to pray with them and for them and remind them that God heals. It never is His precious will for us to suffer, I tell them. Often after a woman finds a breast lump I accompany her to

186

her physician for a complete exam, then to another doctor for a second opinion. I am with her, a "second pair of ears," as the doctors delineate her problem and explain various treatment options.

I am always the first to encourage women (and in a few cases, men) with breast cancer to explore every possible avenue and state-of-the-art treatment today's medicine can provide. But there may be softer alternatives to our heroic modern medicines and treatments that they also deserve to know about. Whenever I am asked, I'll tell other women like me how to find some of those resources. I may explain, for example, why it is advisable to add antioxidants and green foods to one's diet to counter some of the aftereffects of standard radiation therapy or chemotherapy—well-proven information few doctors routinely offer.

I believe strongly in alternative medicine. It can be a Godsend. But I believe in using alternative treatments only as an adjunct to conventional medicine, with rare exceptions. We should select all of our treatment methods carefully and prayerfully, with ongoing gratitude to God for the benefits they provide.

Fourteen

Continuing the Journey

ALTERNATIVE MEDICINE'S TECH-
niques and treatments may be as
broad-spectrum as conventional
medicine's drugs, therapies and
protocols. Some alternatives
include visualization techniques,
massage, acupuncture, chelation
therapy, biofeedback, herbal
remedies, colonics, nutritional
supplements and other well-
known natural therapies and
medicinals.

The advantages are that these
methods often provide safer,
more effective—and even far less

costly—cures than conventional medicine's usual drug-based approaches. There is increasing scientific evidence that many alternative therapies work and are both valid and safe.

Indeed, the trend toward safer, more effective natural cures has led our National Institute of Health and other prestigious research centers to pursue more evidence about the benefits from some of these ancient remedies.

It is important to select only the best from this banquet spread of available natural treatments. Look for those backed by solid research. Is your alternative treatment of choice currently used at teaching hospitals and healthcare facilities? Do the herbal and dietary supplements you are considering provide standardized dosages, allowing you to take the same number of milligrams each time?

If you feel that mainstream medicine has failed to hit the target in treating your particular case, you might want to explore some alternatives. The Internet and various well-known publications, including such prestigious medical journals as *The New England Journal of Medicine, Lancet* and *The Journal of the American Medical Association*, to name just a few, publish articles concerning advances in the alternative medicine world.

But you will have to do your homework . . . a lot of homework. Is it worth it? Countless numbers of people who have attained "miracle cures" after turning to alternative therapies are convinced. Their persistence paid off.

Persistence paid off for me, too. I believe the alternative treatments I chose for myself have proven themselves through the years. Certainly they have done no harm.

I believe, on the contrary, that they have been as fully important to my health and well-being as anything else God has provided.

But there are some cautions to observe when entering the alternative medicine or treatment arena. There are some wacky and unproven "cures" out there. Here again, as with conventional medicine, it's up to us to do our due diligence when our health is at stake. It is my responsibility to sift the wheat from the chaff, examine the evidence and make intelligent choices.

Alternative medicine truly has much to offer. These days conventional medicine is catching on to that fact, and more and more physicians are embracing some very old and well-proved therapies—not only for their patients, but also for themselves.

Reaching Out

When God began sending woman to me who had serious health questions—often about breast cancer—again and again I recalled what my mother had told me: "My mantle will fall on you. You will help people all over the world."

My mother really did minister. So often I wondered where she found the time, the strength and the patience. She always seemed vitally interested in the other person and his or her story. She would listen so attentively, wipe a few tears from her bright eyes and then go into prayer for that person. She would pray down heaven—and her prayers got answered. There was just something about Mother's prayers I felt sure I didn't have.

One day Kay, the fabulous interior designer who had decorated the Mickie Gee Fireside Room and Garden at church, got in touch with me. Actually, we stayed in touch, because I referred her to several other clients for decorating jobs after she completed Mother's magnificent and very special place.

"Dee, I have breast cancer," Kay said in that funny, flat, colorless voice with which women announce the worst news they've ever received.

"Honey! I'm on my way over!" I shouted. I just left my desk the way it was and went. Kay was like me. She had no idea of what breast cancer might involve, what lay ahead, how sick she might become—nothing. So I took her to the doctor. (That's important. Breast cancer patients should have a friend with them when they visit their doctors.) Afterward we discussed what he had told her. Lots of times the doctor's words get mixed up in your mind, so it's good to replay them immediately when you and your friend leave the office.

Kay and I became the *Gold Dust Twins.* I went with

her when she got her second doctor's opinion. I checked on her a lot during her treatments. I taught her everything about nutrition—and she thrived. Today Kay is healed and speaks to women's groups. God has used Kay's breast cancer to give her an important new outreach to help others.

I realized He was doing the same thing for me. The pastor's wife had recommended Kay to me when we designed my mother's memorial room in the church. Frankly, I wasn't too enthusiastic at the time. I'd much prefer to hire my own decorator. But Kay came to my house with her swatches and color samples, and right away we clicked. The room she designed displays all the elegance and grace anyone could want. I fell in love with Kay and her talents.

Could it be, I now wondered, that God, who knew all along about my ministry-to-be and Kay's upcoming breast cancer, had planned for me to encourage her, even walk her through the process of battling her cancer? And did He know how much I wanted her to win? How I prayed for her to win?

Through my experience with Kay and some other breast cancer patients at that time, I began to catch on to that indefinable something Mother had possessed. I saw it was her divine gift of love that had carried her supernaturally through those tough, long, hard-working sessions with so many hurting people.

Love not unlike that which she showered on Daddy and us kids, I reflected. At home Mother was so humble and sweet, so unfailingly, unconditionally loving, always such a lady, courteous to a fault.

Even when I whacked off the pigtails of that mean girl who sat in front of me in grammar school—an act my appalled mother absolutely could not understand—yes, even at times like that she could love me and somehow manage to bring out the best in my hurting and usually unrepentant little heart.

Now I realized something electrifying. God must have literally overflowed my tiny mother at those times when she ministered to others with such patience and power. She did not get tired, for He constantly supplied her, and the power was Love. Love Himself! She had said this same power would fall on me.

Then came Janet, who rushed straight to her doctor when she first felt her lump. "Come back in three months, and we'll check it," he advised.

"Oh no, Janet! No way! Hold on a minute," I ordered her. Putting her line on hold, I dialed Dr. Peters.

"I know you like a book. You have eighty-five patients in your waiting room, but I'm getting Janet's things, and we'll be . . ."

"Here in an hour," George Peters finished. He knows me like a book. He even finishes my sentences.

A little more than an hour later, we learned that Janet had very aggressive cancer. Had she waited three months, it almost certainly would have cost her life. Once again, I felt such awe when I considered how

God Himself loved Janet so much He had guided me to make that phone call to Dr. Peters.

And I understood then, that if I would walk with Him the way my mother always had, He would help me with the words to pray, the energy to serve and the insights and knowledge needed to help the frightened and grief-stricken cancer patients He so loved.

I began to glimpse the true Power within love. I understood that I could minister to and comfort those in need, for the God of love would guide me as I gave His love to others. My arms could wrap around hurting people for His sake.

Deborah, a young mother of two small children, had cancer throughout her reproductive organs. Following extensive surgery, the doctors told her and her husband that with chemotherapy, Deborah might survive—for three months or so.

The devastated little couple showed up at my office that day. Such a sad story, such a terrible, tragic ending ahead for them . . . but that's not what I felt. "I'm going to ask you a question," I began. "Will you do everything I suggest?"

Two pairs of eyes looked up at me, startled. "Because unless you're in this 100 percent, let's don't even start," I emphasized. "Don't whine. Don't tell me something tastes bad. Don't ever tell me you can't do it."

This was not the tone and certainly not the words I would have selected. The couple, however, was looking a little excited. I saw hope beginning to dawn across their faces. Without planning it, suddenly I was dialing a beeper number, hoping to reach an alternative medicine practitioner who had no ordinary telephone. He responded immediately. He would see the young couple.

The afternoon before Thanksgiving Day the pair and myself went to him for Deborah's examination and consultation. They emerged four hours later, loaded with instructions, excitement and with hope now replacing their despair.

That was two years ago. When Deborah refused chemotherapy and informed her doctors that she had decided to try some alternative treatments, they called her an idiot and warned her that she would be dead within three months.

Today she is strong as an ox and too busy to return to that doctor's office to prove she was right. Chemotherapy, for her, was not the treatment of choice.

Fresh Anointing

The month of October had arrived, and with it, an invitation to speak to the student body of Oral Roberts University as one of the featured speakers at the annual Ladies' Conference.

Only weeks earlier, on August 1, I had had that awesome experience in the California hotel room where I had wept and prayed all night while Glenn, unaware, slept in the adjoining room. That night God allowed my heart to be broken by the sufferings of the sick and needy. Visions of that Mexican hospital with its rooms filled with the dying . . . taking those pitiful ill ones into my arms . . . begging the doctors to assure me that they would live . . . That had been a watershed development in my life, I realized. I did not know why it had happened, but I somehow understood that I had been chosen during those hours when I struggled before God—chosen for His service. Trembling, I had said, "Yes, Lord."

What had it all meant? What, exactly, had I said yes to? I wished I could ask my mother. I felt sure she would know. But whenever I thought back to August 1, it all seemed as inexplicable as when it was happening.

How strange, too, that Glenn was not there. How amazing that he could be sleeping soundly in the next room, unaware of my prayers and ceaseless weeping. Except for short business trips, Glenn and I do not separate. I could not remember another time when we had. We are so close we seem like two parts of one person. Glenn says we think alike.

At night he reads to me while I doze off to sleep. He tucks me in. Ordinarily he would be acutely aware if I slipped out of bed and went into another room. Glenn would know I was missing.

Yes, I felt quite sure that God had orchestrated that extraordinary night and all that led up to it. Once we returned home, however, everything seemed familiar and ordinary. It was as though when we left the waves crashing on the beach, we also left behind all the drama and conflict I had known during that unforgettable night.

I had said, "Yes, Lord," so probably that's why I agreed to speak to this large audience—in a small act of obedience. But touching up my face and hair in the ladies' room nearest the auditorium, I noticed something. All the young ladies were wearing dresses. I seemed to be the only person wearing a pants suit.

"Uh, oh," I muttered, "you must have some kind of dress code here."

"Yes," one pretty co-ed agreed. "You can't wear pants in the auditorium during services."

"That's great!" I responded. "I'm your speaker today!"

Behind the chapel stage, we all held hands, then walked out together. I stepped to the podium. "Whoops! I've really blown this," I announced. "President Richard Roberts asked me to come speak to you, and I showed up in pants.

"I blew it on my very first try!"

The students roared. They loved it. And from then on, the meeting was electric.

When the meeting let out one hour later, I felt that same solemn feeling, that absolute quiet I had felt in our hotel room as morning burst forth following my night of tears. The feeling cannot be described.

The next day at the Ladies' Conference I just told my testimony, preceded by much prayer. There surely was no reason to feel nervous. Glenn was there. The people from our company's laboratory had flown in to hear me speak. And my friend Marian Barnes sat in the front row near Cheryl Pruitt Salem, a former Miss America, who is our friend.

This was something new for me. The lights, cameras and audience—and me alone on stage.

Then I was speaking of my mother and her godliness, and of my father who taught me the books of the Bible when I was a tiny little girl. I was sharing how Daddy spent his money on cute dresses for Sandra and me, and of the only luxury he ever bought himself—an occasional bottle of Old Spice.

I was realizing how strongly goodness and mercy and the love of God had run like a strong river that watered the lives of us all. I saw God's pure goodness in my husband's face and in the faces of my friends and the many other men and women of God gathered there that day.

And then it was time for the altar call. Something I had told God I simply could not do. I can pray with you one on one, but pray in public? There was no hesitation whatsoever. The Holy Spirit brought one after another to His altar for prayer.

Once again, I met the living God as I had met Him in that distant hotel room. And at last, I understood the source of mother's powerful prayer ministry. She operated under the awesome empowering of the God of the universe. At that moment I realized at last, with

198

utter finality, that it was finished. I would never return to the woman I had been. I had said "Yes, Lord," and like my mother, I could never turn back.

As I continue this journey, I wish to leave you with one message: One of the greatest blessings God can give to you is the gift of someone who cares. Dee Simmons truly cares. My commitment is, and always will be, to save lives.

Laugh often; love much!

1-800-360-0988

Ultimate Living's
nutritional product line includes:

Green Miracle—health-food store in a can; equal to 5
servings of fruits and vegetables;
immune enhancer.

Multivitamin—complete foundation of your nutritional
program; includes 400 IU vitamin E.

Super Antioxidant (150 mg)—20 to 50 times more
powerful than vitamins C and E.

Cal-Mag Plus—Hydroxyapatite Calcium/Magnesium;
assists in the prevention of bone loss.

Fiber Cleanse—flushes out the body's toxins and waste;
promotes colon health.

Men's Formula—addresses men's specific needs; promotes prostate health.

Ionic Trace Minerals—replaces all trace minerals
missing in our diets.

Ezzeac Plus Tea With Cat's Claw—immune-strengthening
herbal tea.

Arthritis Formula—complete bone, joint and ligament
health supplement.

Breast Cream—promotes early detection of breast disease.

Harmony Cream—highest pharmaceutical grade of
natural progesterone and wild yam.

Natural Deodorant—all natural; contains no alu-
minum; essential for healthy protection.

Ultimate Living's
complete skin-care products include:

Hydrating Cleanser (normal to dry)—cleanses and nourishes the skin with pure essential oils.

Cleansing Gel (normal to oily)—controls oil and break-outs; clears away makeup and impurities.

Balancing Toner—restores pH balance of the skin; leaves skin revitalized.

Anti-Aging Complex—firms, tightens sagging skin; combats premature aging and fine lines.

Enriched Moisturizer (normal to dry)—restores moisture balance to the skin.

Oil-Free Moisturizer (normal to oily)—a lightweight, oil-free moisturizer.

Hydrating Oil—nourishes and hydrates dry skin; restores skin's youthful glow.

Skin Renewal Mask—gently exfoliates and renews skin texture.

Hand and Body Creme—natural and organic; gives maximum moisture levels.

For more information on Ultimate Living's nutritional supplements and skin-care products, write to:

ULTIMATE LIVING INTERNATIONAL, INC.
P. O. Box 191326
Dallas, Texas 75219
214-220-1240

Or, you can contact us at Ultimate Living's Web site:

www.ultimateliving.com

Pick up these other health-related
books from Siloam Press:

Maximum Energy
BY TED BROER

Walking in Divine Health
BY DON COLBERT, M.D.

You Are Not What You Weigh
BY LISA BEVERE

The Bible Cure
BY REGINALD CHERRY, M.D.

Healthy Expectations
BY PAMELA SMITH

Fit for Excellence!
BY SHERI ROSE SHEPHERD

The Hope of Living Cancer Free!
BY FRANCISCO CONTRERAS, M.D.

Train Up Your Children in the Way They Should Eat
BY SHARON BROER

Bible Cure Booklets
BY DON COLBERT, M.D.

Available at your local bookstore
or call 1-800-599-5750
or visit our Web site at www.creationhouse.com